Better Homes
& Gardens

celebrate the
SEASON
2020

contents

fall

trims

food

gifts

120 Nothing shows more sentiment than something made by hand. Pour your love into do-it-yourself projects to bring cheer to everyone on your gift list. Organizers, serving accessories, tasty treats, and more are included in this chapter that offers extraordinary gift ideas.

kids

140 Include children when bringing your holiday home to life. Their artistic talents will shine with paint, pompoms, buttons, and papers transformed into fun projects like cupcake toppers, tree ornaments, treat holders, and gift trims. What a fun way to share time together!

in a twinkling

Enjoy making striking seasonal decorations that can be done in the wink of an eye.

MEREDITH CONSUMER MARKETING
Director of Direct Marketing-Books: Daniel Fagan
Marketing Operations Manager: Max Daily
Assistant Marketing Manager: Kylie Dazzo
Senior Production Manager: Liza Ward

WATERBURY PUBLICATIONS, INC.
Editorial Director: Lisa Kingsley
Creative Director: Ken Carlson
Associate Editor: Tricia Bergman
Associate Design Director: Doug Samuelson
Assistant Editor: Will Bortz
Production Assistant: Mindy Samuelson
Contributing Editor: Sue Banker
Contributing Copy Editor: Terri Fredrickson
Contributing Proofreader: Joleen First
Contributing Food Stylist: Jennifer Peterson

BETTER HOMES & GARDENS® MAGAZINE
Editor in Chief: Stephen Orr
Executive Editor: Oma Blaise Ford
Creative Director: Jennifer D. Madara

MEREDITH CORPORATION
President and CEO: Tom Harty
Chairman: Stephen M. Lacy
Vice Chairman: Mell Meredith Frazier

Cheers to the Seasons!

There is something beautiful about every season. Whether it is spring's awakening of Mother Nature, the summer's beckoning sun, the fall's miraculous colors, or winter's peaceful wonderland, each offers a reason to celebrate. The holiday season, full of hope and wonder, holds a place of honor on that list.

Better Homes & Gardens® Celebrate the Season® joins in the fun with dozens of can-do ideas to make this much anticipated time of the year unforgettable.

Have fun discovering awesome DIY projects to make your home a welcoming haven filled with holiday cheer. Enjoy cooking delicious kitchen-tested recipes sure to impress family and friends. Bring smiles to everyone on your gift list with amazing surprises—made-by-hand treasures that share your creativity and love. And right along with you, young ones will delight in making seasonal trims using easy-on-the-budget supplies.

As you embrace the upcoming seasons filled with thanksgiving and merriment, we hope you're inspired by these pages, finding beautiful ways to share the spirit of the season with all the special people in your life.

May comfort and joy fill your heart throughout every season.

Lu Barker

fall

AUTUMNAL DELIGHT
Honor the season with fun-to-make projects fitting of its splendor.

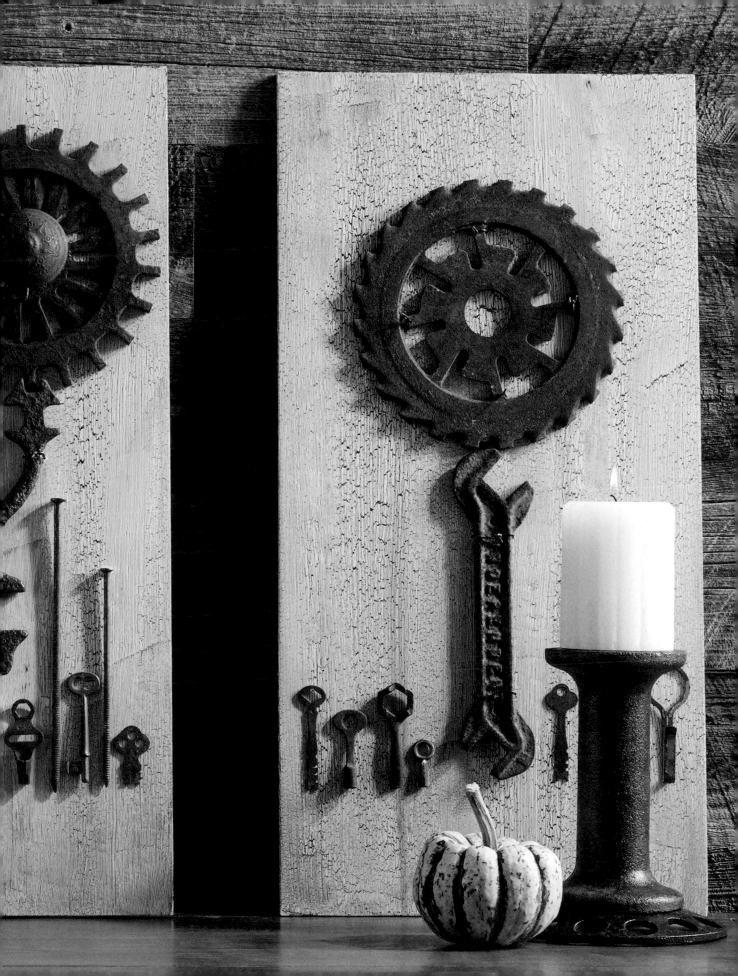

Faux the Home

Capture the glory of this season of thanks with everlasting blooms, berries, and leaves leading the way.

PERSONAL POSIES

Simple place cards transform into elegant table dressings with the addition of sprigs of faux flowers, leaves, and berries. For each card, pen a name right of center on a folded piece of cardstock. Hot-glue grouped faux pieces to the left of each name. For longer names, move the mini arrangement closer to the corner of the card.

EARTHY WELCOME

A grapevine wreath dons a gorgeous coat of autumnal bliss with mauve leaves peeking through with unexpected flecks of contrasting light. Choose flowers, leaves, and berries in fall colors and warm-tone metallic; trim off excess stems using wire cutters. To give the wreath balance, start by placing large flower heads evenly spaced around the wreath; wire or glue the blooms in place. Fill in the wreath with leaves, berries, and a multiloop bow with trailing tails.

GRACED

Embellish each guest's place setting with a gorgeous focal point. Shape the wire stem of a large faux bloom into a circle, approximately 1½ to 2 inches in diameter; snip off excess stem with a wire cutter. Hot-glue leaves and berries to the underside of the petals to complete the napkin ring.

FRUITFUL FAVORS

Send Thanksgiving guests home with a jar of goodies to tell them how grateful you are for them. This jar already had a decorative wood lid, but you could easily use a woodburning tool to share your own message. Hot-glue faux naturals to one side as the finishing touch to this gift of thanks.

LIVING ON THE EDGE

Plate chargers get decked out for the season with the addition of a mini bouquet adorning one side. Keeping the foliage to one edge so as not to interrupt the placement of a dinner plate, hot-glue the larger leaves in place first. Adhere flowers in the center with berry sprigs on each side.

ARTFUL ARRANGEMENT

A candlelit lantern is pretty in itself, but open its door to include a waterfall of cattails, leaves, berries, and flowers for an even more beautiful seasonal sensation. Use a battery-operated candle for safety; one with a remote or timer allows candlelight without having to disrupt the arrangement.

BANDED BASKETS

Single servings get special delivery treatment when served in ornamented baskets. Coat the rim of each mini basket with paint in an autumnal hue. When dry, hot-glue a small bouquet to one corner. Fill a treat bag with pistachios, or other snack, and close with a metallic twist tie and a gift tag.

Rust to Riches

The time-kissed patina of rusted metal lends old-world charm to tabletops and walls. Before using them, wash pieces to remove excess rust.

FIRMLY PLANTED

Crackled paint provides a textured background for an artistic arrangement of gears, wrenches, doorknobs, keys, and more.

WHAT YOU NEED

16×24-inch piece of ½-inch thick plywood for each picture
Acrylic paint in brown and ivory
Foam brush
Hide glue, such as Titebond
Clear acrylic topcoat spray, if desired
Rusted metal components, such as gears, discs, machinery parts, doorknobs, wrenches, keys, and nails
Pencil
Drill and small bit
Strong wire
Wire cutter
Needle-nose pliers
Instant glue, such as CA Glue

WHAT YOU DO

1. Paint each board brown as shown in Photo A; let dry.
2. Paint an even coat of Hide glue onto each board as shown in Photo B; let dry. The surface will remain shiny.
3. Paint the entire surface ivory. The paint will begin to crackle as you paint as shown in Photo C. Let the paint dry. Spray with topcoat, if desired, and let dry.
4. Arrange the metal components into a floral design using the photo for inspiration. Use a pencil to mark areas where wire should be inserted to hold the metal pieces in place.
5. Working in one area at a time, drill through the board where marked. If easier, remove each metal piece before drilling an area.
6. Cut pieces of wire long enough to hold metal pieces to the wood. Use the wire to hold each metal piece in place; twist in the front using needle-nose pliers to secure. For small pieces, use instant glue to secure them to the wood.

INSTANTANEOUS

A basket-shape cast-iron piece, such as this hog feeder,
makes a sturdy holder for autumn gourds. To avoid the basket
scratching the tabletop surface, adhere felt or silicone pads to
the bottom.

PICTURESQUE

Display photos, cards, and more on a magnetic grate that lends lovely color and texture to the background. Lightly sand the grate top to create a smooth surface for magnets; wipe away dust. Spray the back with a clear sealer; let dry. Weave strong ribbon through the top of the grate; knot ends for hanging.

"GRATE"NESS

Surround a crafts store mirror with an ornamental grate for a stunning shabby chic home accent. Spray the back with clear sealer; let dry. Depending on the design of the grate, use either a strong multipurpose glue or mirror mounting hardware to attach the mirror to the back of the grate.

SLIPCOVERED

Whether from farming, logging, manufacturing, or other equipment, a tall cast-iron cylinder disguises a bottle, glass, or vase with a rich rust coat. Shown here is a wagon wheel sheath. Choose a plastic or glass vessel insert, straight or flared, that fits easily inside the cylinder. Carefully pour in water and slip on the cover; fill with flowers. Reverse the steps to refresh the water.

TOPSY-TURVY

Cast-iron pieces that nest firmly together make clever candleholders. This disc plow spool and corn planter plate can be flopped to offer two different looks. Before adding a pillar candle, make sure the pieces fit firmly together for safety purposes. *Never leave burning candles unattended.*

KNOBBY

Old doorknobs make wonderfully weighted vases for dried fall sprigs. Use the mini decorations to brighten up small spaces or to use as table favors. Choose knobs with flat fronts so they sit upright. Remove any hardware and fill the shank with short stalks of dried naturals, such as wheat, poppies, and leafy stems.

Dress Up the Table

A table, beautifully set, makes any gathering one for which to be extra grateful. Use these simple ideas to make a grand autumnal presentation.

GOODNESS AND LIGHT

Easily carry autumn's splendor room to room by dressing up a
vintage tin votive tray—or a cupcake pan—with pinecones, glass
votive candles, sprigs of Hypericum berries, and evergreen
clippings. The use of faux greens and berries allows this lovely
arrangement to be enjoyed through winter.

Never leave burning candles unattended.

QUAINT GATHERING

Put your spin on the centerpiece by grouping some of your
favorite pretties. To vary the heights of like items, use time-
kissed books as risers. To pull it all together, fill in the display
with greenery and naturals. Faux fruit adds color without the
care of an expiration date.

SIMPLY GATHERED

Despite the name, centerpieces don't need to be the center of attention. Let them complement the table, not steal the show. Glassware, candles, and autumn clippings are all you need. Start with a tray or platter to define the arrangement. Put large items in the middle and small items toward the ends.

Never leave burning candles unattended.

PERFECT PEAR-INGS

There's no doubt that roses bring a touch of elegance to any scene. Here, the velvety white blooms mingle with seasonal pears and fragrant eucalyptus for a sophisticated setting. A gold charger lends refinement to a simple white plate topped with a cleverly folded napkin and green pear bearing a silver-scripted place card. The gorgeous arrangement—dotted with large silver jingle bells—works its way into the Christmas season as well.

SETTING THE SCENE

A silver charger topped by three plates takes a cue from autumn with a tucked-in chocolate napkin. A spray-painted, hand-glittered, nonedible pear tops the place setting. Embrace the love of an eclectic scene blending copper, mercury, and silver elements. For a stunning centerpiece, start with a snow-white knit tablerunner (opposite) and top with abundant greenery, flocked branches, and paint-kissed pinecones.

BRAID BRIGADE

Revert to the joys of middle school braiding—without the peer pressure. Lengths of cotton rope easily transform into braided rings that can serve as place card wreaths. Starting with three 15-inch lengths of rope, knot together at one end and braid the ropes until 8 inches in length; hot-glue ends together. Form braid into a circle and hot-glue to a 3-inch metal ring. Customize the finishing accents with faux greenery and berries, wood beads, and a paper banner.

EARTHY FAVORITES

Accent your door with a light and airy wreath with showy, long-lasting king protea as the star. The wire base also holds wispy branches of seeded eucalyptus, cypress., Brunia berries, and Leucadendron buds.

Natural Love

Welcome the warmth of nature into your home with magically intoxicating wreaths that make a grand first impression.

PICTURE THIS

An old wooden picture frame is the unexpected base for this rectangular wreath. Look for a heavy frame with sides that are at least 2 inches wide. Use floral wire to attach cuttings. For fullness and dimension, feature a variety of greens—spruce, pine, oregonia, and magnolia leaves (some flipped over so their velvety brown undersides show). Delicate herbs, such as sage and rosemary, are tucked in for softness and fragrance. Bright Berzillia berries are wired in for a finishing touch.

FREE-FORM

A grapevine base anchors tendrils of homey bracelet greenery, plus cuttings of persimmon, thistle, silver Brunia, and eucalyptus nuts. The asymmetrical arrangement adds to this wreath's unique appearance.

SIMPLY DELICIOUS

For an edgier take on wreaths, try a square metal form. This one is covered with several bunches of 4- to 6-inch branches of preserved boxwood to maintain its color. Layer and wire the boxwood onto the frame along with Pittosporum and Victorian birch. Rose hips, apples, and Hypericum are the ruby-red jewels wired and glued in place.

Beautiful in Brown

FLOWER FAVORS

Whether it's Thanksgiving dinner or a casual fall get-together, everyone will love this take-home tribute to the season. Fill small antique or new bottles with dried wheat stalks, flowers, and sticks. Tie each neck with a ribbon bow and place a mini dried bouquet by each guest's place at the table.

FRESH IDEA

Fresh berry stalks bring life to a natural grapevine wreath. Drill two button-style holes in the center of a pair of live-edge wood slices. Thread strong wire through the holes to secure them to the wreath. Reinforce the bond using hot glue. Use instant glue, made for glass and wood, to adhere bottles to the wood slices. Use a funnel to fill bottles with water and add a fresh berry stem to each.

BOTTLE BOTTOM VOTIVE HOLDER

A beer bottle's rich color shines through when made into a seasonal votive holder. Using protective gloves and eyewear, and following the safety instructions from the manufacturer, use a bottle cutter to cut through the beer bottle approximately 3 inches from the bottom. Smooth the rim as directed. Wrap the votive holder with artificial berried vine; glue ends together to secure around glass.

NO ORDINARY ORGANIZER

Keep hobby (and work) areas tidy using jars and bottles as organizers. Snippets of jute and seasonal charms dress up the vessels with ease.

SYRUP BOTTLE REVIVAL

A vintage American syrup bottle makes a fun conversation starter. Trim the top with wraps of jute hot-glued to the glass. The narrow neck makes it easy to fan a spray of wheat and mini cattails.

trims

SPREAD GOOD CHEER
Tap into your creative side to
make your home a holiday
haven for family and friends.

For the Love of Lodge

Winter sports—skating, skiing, sledding, and more—inspire heartfelt, cabin-cozy, vintage decorating.

BEST SEAT IN THE HOUSE
A flexible flyer makes a showy holiday decoration with the addition of a faux wreath. Stain a holiday wood cutout for a striking focal point.

SEASONAL SWAG
Winterize an everyday wall piece with a greenery swag cradling one side. Shape the swag to frame a corner. Enhance the greenery with adornments like these pinecones, jingle bells, rustic wood ski ornaments, and bow.

WINTRY WELCOME

Kids' skis are just the right size to make a cozy door accent. For the base, wire together a pair of worn wood skis; attach a greenery spray to the center and leave a loop on the back for hanging. Complete the door decoration with jingle bells, a double ribbon bow, and a deer ornament crowning the top.

A SHOE-IN

Authentic snowshoes offer vintage flair to holiday decor. Wire a pair of snowshoes together and get them holiday ready with the addition of silk poinsettias, greenery, berries, a premade fabric banner, and a bow. To make your own banner, use iron-on letters and ribbon.

OFF THE SLOPES

Home decor gets a wintry boost with a ski shelf showing off a seasonal collection. Craft a sturdy shelf unit using timeworn skis as side supports. Separated by a trio of 24-inch shelves attached with L brackets, the unit's back is supported with a trio of 8×24-inch boards screwed into the ski backs just below the shelves. Sturdy D hooks, screwed into each ski 1 foot from the tip, keep the shelf firmly against the wall.

CHEERFUL COATRACK

Take your pick of seasonal wood cutouts from a crafts store to top a premade coatrack. Stain the wood design to match the coatrack and let dry. Use wood glue to attach the cutout so it towers above the rack.

A LEG UP

A vintage toboggan transforms into a showy side table to enjoy until the spring blooms pop through the soil. Let the design of the toboggan determine the type of leg brackets to use and attach 28-inch legs to all corners.

CUTE CUFFS

Antique skates, hung from an embellished coatrack, create a charming wall arrangement. For each skate cuff, cut a 15-inch length of 3½-inch-wide piece of wired ribbon. Remove the wire from one edge. Gather the ribbon slightly on the other edge; twist the wire ends together to secure. Sew a contrasting ribbon bow and jingle bell opposite the open ends of the cuff. Place the cuff around a skate top. Put a small plastic cup into the skate and fill with greens and a jumbo candy cane stick.

PLAYFUL BUFFET

Make a lasting impression at your next gathering by staging an atmosphere that's incredibly cozy and welcoming. Anchor the decorating theme with black-and-white buffalo plaid, allowing occasional colors to shine. Enhance the winter sports theme with a framed piece like this vintage calendar page. Magazine covers from winter months and enlarged Christmas cards or postcards also work well.

ORNAMENTAL ACCENT
Candlelight exudes a sense of warmth and calm, and this vignette replicates just that. Place a lantern on a tray and surround it with artificial greens. Tuck in a couple of retro ornaments for an arrangement that's merry and bright.

SWEET RIDE
Sweet treats rise to the occasion arranged on a sled serving board. Avoid table scratches by cushioning the sled with a tablerunner or adhere felt strips to the bottom.

FREESTYLE
Grouping a variety of winter sports pieces continues the theme. A pair of skates, hung from red laces and filled with seasonal picks, makes a spirited accompaniment hung near a vintage print.

Devine Inspiration

Glorify the meaning of Christmas through heavenly strokes of paint.

ANGEL WE HAVE HEARD ON HIGH

Colorful paint and snow white dots come together to make a vibrant angel.

WHAT YOU NEED

16×20-inch artist canvas

Acrylic paint in desired colors, plus black and white

Large flat and medium rounded paintbrushes

Tracing paper

Pencil

Scissors

Pointed rubber-tipped colour shaper tools

WHAT YOU DO

1. Paint the canvas black; let dry.

2. Trace the face pattern, page 152; cut out. With the chin centered left to right and 7 inches down from the canvas top edge, trace around the pattern onto the canvas as shown in Photo A.

3. Paint the face with desired flesh color and blushed cheeks as shown in Photo B. While the paint is wet and using the photo for inspiration, use a shaper tool to "draw in" the eyes, nose, mouth, and eyebrows (removing the paint) as shown in Photo C.

4. Paint in lip color as shown in Photo D.

5. Paint the hair, halo, and hands as shown in Photos E, F, and G.

6. Paint in wing shapes and robe using sweeping strokes as shown in Photo H. Use the photo as an example on changing colors.

7. To paint snow, dip a pencil eraser into white paint and dot onto the surface as shown in Photo I. Dip the handle end of a paintbrush into white paint to make small dots between the wing and robe paint swirls.

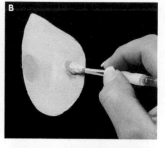

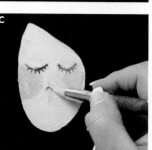

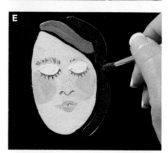

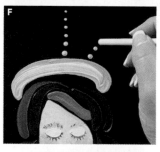

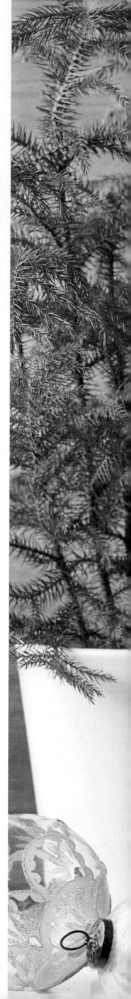

AWAY IN A MANGER

Handmade cards are so appreciated, and this design is frameable. Fold a 5½×11-inch piece of white cardstock in half, aligning the short ends. Trace the baby's head pattern on page 152; cut out. Trace around the pattern on a 5-inch square of black cardstock, centered left to right and with the chin 1¾ inches from the bottom edge. Paint in the head using desired flesh tone. Use a small rounded paintbrush to make two sweeping strokes to resemble a blanket. Add hay using sweeping strokes of gold, yellow, and white. Let the paint dry. Dip the paintbrush handle into yellow paint to make the halo and "+" section of a star. Dip the handle in white paint to accent the halo, hay, and star as shown; let dry. Use double-sided tape to back the painted piece; trim a narrow border. Mount on one side of the folded card.

DECK THE HALLS

Set your holiday table with simply painted 2×4-inch canvases guiding guests to their places. For each place card, paint a mini canvas black; let dry. Paint or use a marking pen to write the guest's first initial in the center of the canvas. Brush short strokes of green/white and teal/white or purple/white paint in the formations shown. Dip the tip of the paintbrush handle into white/pink paint and dot onto the surface to resemble berries; let dry. Place the canvas on a mini easel and top with a sprig of greenery.

O' TANNENBAUM

Three colors of paint and small paper pieces is all it takes to make gift tags for all your holiday packages. Cut a 3-inch square of black cardstock. Mark the center of the card, ¼ inch from the bottom edge. Dip the tip of a paintbrush handle into white paint and dot onto the cardstock where marked. Continue making dots vertically without reloading the paint to make smaller dots moving upward. Brush short strokes of green/white to make stylized tree branches as shown. Dot the top with yellow/white for a star. Let the paint dry. Use double-sided tape to back the painted piece with gold glitter paper; trim a narrow border. Use tape to adhere the design to a 3¾×7½-inch piece of cardstock folded in half.

Paper Hooray

Papers in holiday prints are an inexpensive way to make a grand impression—from cards sent through the mail to trims on the tree and the packages underneath it.

STOCKING FAVORS

Paper stockings deliver sweet treats with whimsy. Trace the patterns on page 153; cut out. Use patterns to cut out a pair of stocking pieces plus one heel and cuff. Align all pieces; use a glue stick to hold cuff and heel to the stocking piece.

Use a small paper punch to make holes approximately ½ inch around the edge and ¼ inch in from the edge. Punch a hole 1 inch in from corner to attach and a second one just above the cuff edge to use for pompoms. Thread a darning needle with yarn; stitch together, weaving needle under and over as shown in Photo A.

When stitching is complete, stitch again to make a stitching line solid as shown in Photo B. Add a hanging loop to the right corner of the stocking.

To make pom-poms, wrap a ruler approximately 30 times with yarn, leaving long tails as shown in Photo C. Slide the wrapped yarn off the ruler as shown in Photo D; tie in the center tightly with an 8-inch piece of yarn. Clip loops and trim ends even with pom-pom. Separate a single white wired faux berry; poke it into the center of the pom-pom and through a punched hole in the stocking. Fold over the wire and tape in place.

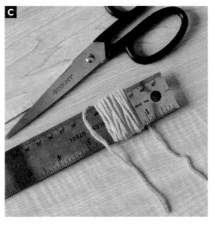

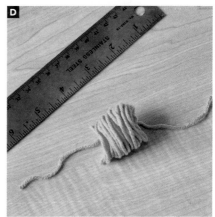

TAG A BAG

A tag-shape punch makes it easy to create gift tags year-round. Punch out a tag from white cardstock. Use a glue stick to adhere the cutout to patterned holiday paper; trim even with the sides and leave some pattern showing at each end. Punch a hole through both layers at the top of the tag shape. Adhere a dimensional sticker as the finishing touch.

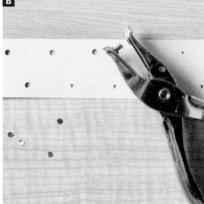

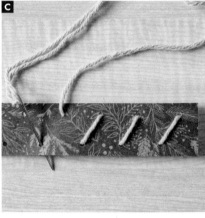

IT'S A WRAP

A cylinder vase gets a seasonal disguise with a tritone paper sleeve. Cut the bottom paper strip long enough to wrap around the vase by approximately two-thirds of the height. Cut the top piece one-third of the height. Cut the center band 1 inch wide. Use a pencil to mark holes 1 inch apart and ¼ inch from the edge. Mark holes on the opposite edge, shifting ½ inch as shown in Photo A. Punch through the marks as shown in Photo B. Thread a darning needle with yarn. Make straight stitches in one direction as shown in Photo C, then the other to create a zigzag as shown in Photo D. Place a piece of double-sided tape vertically on the vase. Wrap the vase with the paper, using the tape to hold the paper seams.

SNOW FOLKS

Invite friendly faces to spruce up holiday giftwrapping. Trace patterns, page 152; cut out. Use patterns to cut pieces from scrapbook papers. Use a paper punch to make holes for stitching. Thread a darning needle with yarn; backstitch through holes. Punch holes at scarf bottoms; fringe with yarn as shown in Photo A. Trim ends even as shown in Photo B. Use a glue stick to adhere pieces together. Back design with black paper; trim a narrow border. Use a white paint marker to add highlights; let dry. Punch a hole at the top; thread with yarn.

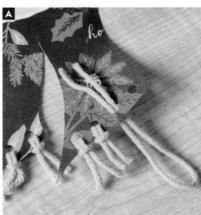

RUN AROUND

A plain white hatbox becomes a Christmas sensation with patterned paper and long running stitches of yarn. Cut a paper band, piecing if necessary, to wrap the box bottom, leaving the lid overlap uncovered. Using a bowl or plate slightly smaller than the lid, trace around it on paper; cut out using decorative-edge scissors. Punch holes around edge of paper, approximately ¾ inch in from edge and 1 inch apart. Thread a darning needle with a double strand of yarn long enough to wrap around hatbox. Sew running stitches through punched holes; knot ends and trim even. Use a glue stick to adhere the decorative paper to the box top. Glue a chipboard embellishment to the center of the lid.

FAUX SEW

Paper circles, punched button-style, make child's play out of this greeting card design. Use a 1¼-inch punch to cut seven buttons and a 1½-inch punch to cut a backing circle for each button. Thread a darning needle with yarn; stitch Xs through the button shapes. Hot-glue the buttons to the backing pieces. Cut a 5½×11-inch piece of cardstock; fold with short edge aligned. Cut a 4×5-inch piece and a 1½×½-inch trunk from white cardstock. Use a glue stick to adhere white cardstock to card front, centering left to right and placing ½ inch from top. Punch holes in a row lengthwise; back-stitch with yarn. Hot-glue the stem at the bottom edge of the card, centered left to right. Use a glue stick to adhere the white cardstock to the card, 1⅛ inches from the bottom. Hot-glue the buttons in triangular formation and top with a chipboard star.

Clay Play

Favorite cookie cutter shapes and simple tools work their magic on
layered and marbled oven-baked clay.

HIDDEN AGENDA

A simple carving in an evergreen pattern reveals color from
below. Cover work surface with waxed paper. Use a rolling
pin to roll out ¼-inch-thick slabs of oven-bake clay in green
and white. Layer the slabs; roll until the layers together are
approximately ¼ inch thick. Use a fluted circle cookie cutter to
cut out the shape. Using the photo as a guide, remove the top
layer with a wire loop tool and exposing the green underneath.
Use a pencil to poke three divots into the ornament. Roll small
balls of red clay, place in ornament, impress with pencil tip. Use
a small straw to make a hole in the top of the ornament. Bake
the ornament in the oven as directed by the manufacturer.

DANCING STARS

The fun part of marbleizing clay is that each pattern is unique.
To marbleize clay, roll ropes of white clay and gold clay. Twist
the ropes together; shape into a coil. Place the clay on waxed
paper. Use a rolling pin to flatten the clay into ¼-inch thickness.
Use a star-shape cookie cutter to cut shapes from clay. From
the scraps, roll marble-size beads, using a straw to make the
holes in the center. Bake the clay pieces in the oven as directed
by the manufacturer. String the beads and stars on cord; knot
between shapes.

CUT IT OUT

Topping wrapped gifts or hanging from Christmas tree branches, golden bells bring a sense of charming nostalgia. To make a trim, cover the work surface with waxed paper; use a rolling pin to roll out ¼-inch-thick slabs of oven-bake clay in white and metallic gold. Layer the gold slab on the white; roll until the layers together are approximately ¼ inch thick. Use a bell-shape cookie cutter to cut out the shape; remove excess. Use a wire loop tool to accent the bell. To make dots, use a pencil point. For the clapper, roll a pea-size ball from white clay; press into place. Use a pencil to accent the clapper. Use a straw to make a hole for hanging. Bake the ornament in oven as directed by the manufacturer.

STAINED-GLASS CHURCH ORNAMENT

Cover the work surface with waxed paper. Break off several small pieces of oven-bake clay in green, blue, purple, and red. Roll the clay pieces into a ball; flatten. Use a rolling pin to roll out the clay into a ¼-inch-thick slab. Roll a ¼-inch-thick slab of white clay. Layer the white slab over the multicolor slab; roll into a ¼-inch-thick slab. Use a church-shape cookie cutter to cut out the shape. Carve out arched windows and a door. Use a pencil point to outline the windows and door and to add a cross above the door. Impress the pencil tip along the roof edge. Snip a loop off a paper clip; press the cut ends into the top of the ornament. Bake the clay in oven as directed by the manufacturer.

Glorious Ruby Red

Paired with green and white, glass in brilliant red completes the traditional Christmastime color scheme.

FACES OF VASES

Light glows through red transparent glass for a stunning display no matter if the vase is vintage or dollar-store variety.

BUCKLE UP

A rhinestone-studded buckle dresses up a vase in seconds. Wrap the vase with wide coordinating ribbon and thread the ends through the buckle.

SILVER SHELL

Gilded flakes, available in crafts stores, add a rich metallic sheen to the surface of the glass. Following the manufacturer's directions, brush on glue in a wavy pattern on the bottom half of the vase. Apply flakes sparingly, allowing some of the red glass to show through. Let dry as directed by the manufacturer.

GLOW FOR IT

Red glass shines naturally, and with a little help, it can glow and sparkle, too. To add flickers of light, drape fine-wired string lights inside the vessel.

BEAUTIFUL BOW

A bellowing bow becomes even more sophisticated with a sparkling brooch pinned to its center.

BEJEWELED

For a quick sparkling accent, use jewelry in lieu of a bow. Simply drape ruby red beaded necklaces around the vase, accompanied by other sensations, such as pearls and strands in silver and gold.

SINGLE SERVING.

Send guests home with a ruby red votive candleholder. As an unexpected surprise, fill with a delicious piece of candy in a paper liner. Trim a small segment from a thin piece of ribbon. Hot-glue a decorative button or pin to the left side. Once the candy is gone, the mini glass cup can shine bright with a votive candle tucked inside.

FESTIVE FAVORS

Lantern-style candleholders become pretty treat carriers. Trim
the handle with a short piece of ribbon and a sprig of greenery.
Line the candleholder with paper shred and fill with candies.

LOVELY LAYERS

Marbles catch the light for a glistening display. Place a white pillar candle in the center of a clear glass candleholder. Fill in around the candle with a layer of clear marbles, then red, and a top layer of clear.

ALL DRESSED UP

Layered ribbons topped with a rhinestone button add simple elegance to ordinary candleholders. Use hot glue to hold the trims in place.

Never leave burning candles unattended.

CENTER OF ATTENTION

A holiday wreath is the perfect nesting place for a ruby red
garden globe. Surround the main attraction with frosted
pinecones and silver jingle bells.

Trims

Accordion-fold a napkin and pin the folds together with a brooch. Fresh greens complete the dinner party presentation.

AMONGST GEMS

Old-fashioned drinking glasses do double duty as candleholders; the cut glass is all the decoration they need. Placed in a gem-filled silver tray, the candle collection shines bright.

Never leave burning candles unattended.

WITH CHARACTER

Wrapping paper characters become treasured ornaments framed in circles of silver and gold. Cut a 4½-inch circle from lightweight cardboard. Brush one side with decoupage medium; center a wrapping paper motif over circle and press onto glue. Trim the excess and let dry. Hot-glue a 4-inch silver ring on top of design. Trim around the ring with gold chenille stem. Trim the lower left corner with faux greenery sprigs and a double ribbon bow. Hot-glue a ribbon loop on the back side for hanging.

Scrap Wrap

Rescue scraps and tail ends of holiday wrapping paper for all sorts of easy-on-the-budget projects.

WORTH REPLEATING

Retro to elegant, whimsical to farmhouse—the look of this trim changes easily with paper choice and color scheme. For each pleated trim, cut three 7-inch-square pieces from wrapping paper. Accordion-fold each piece every ¾ inch; fold in half. Use a glue stick to adhere the ends of the three pleated sections together to form a circle. Trace a 2¼-inch circle on the back of desired cardstock; cut out using pinking shears. Hot-glue the circle in the center of the pleated ornament; top with a contrasting jingle bell. To hang, hot-glue a string end in the crease of a pleat on the back side of the ornament.

FIRST IMPRESSION

Decorative tags make a playful stand-in for a door wreath. Use decoupage medium to adhere coordinating wrapping paper to a pair of 12-inch-long heavy cardboard tags. Hot-glue metallic gold chenille stems around the edges and holes, piecing if necessary. Trim the front tag with chipboard lettering, sticker letters, and holiday pins with the backs removed. Thread a piece of ribbon through the holes. Overlap the tags as desired; hot-glue together. Drill a couple of tiny holes at the top of each tag; thread with wire and twist around wreath to secure in place.

CAN DO

Create a jolly holiday arrangement using a peanut can as a base. Cover the can with wrapping paper, using double-sided tape to adhere it in place. Hot-glue ribbon trim around both the top and bottom edges. Ribbon loops and jingle bells accent the rim.

SPRINKLING OF JOY

Bring joy to the table with a sprinkling of merry characters, holiday phrases, and seasonal hues. To make confetti, use a glue stick to adhere leftover wrapping-paper scraps to cardstock. Cut out shapes using small circle punches. For flecks of sparkle, punch a few shapes from gold glitter cardstock.

SEASONAL SNIPPETS

An inexpensive brass napkin ring gets dressed for the holiday season with a temporary band of wrapping paper. Use double-sided tape to adhere the paper to the ring. Cut a narrow strip of tape to hold narrow ribbon perpendicular to the paper band. The elements can be easily redone for the next season.

IN-A-JIFFY GIFT TAGS
Rescue the best parts of wrapping-paper remnants to make gift tags in all
sizes. Cut out the designs, back with glitter paper, and trim a narrow border.
Adhere the layered piece to a folded piece of white cardstock.

CHRISTMAS TREE GREETING CARD

These dimensional cards will bring glad tidings wherever they land. Cut three 8-inch-long triangles from wrapping paper; 1 inch, 2 inch and 3 inches at the wide ends. For each scroll, start with the wide end and roll up; use a glue stick to hold the end down. Cut a 3¾×5¾-inch piece of cardstock. Cut a 5-inch piece of ¼-inch-wide ribbon; hot-glue it on the cardstock; place it in the center. Glue the smallest bead 1¼ inch from the top, the other two beads 1 inch apart. Cut a ¾-inch circle for the star; glue at the top and hot-glue a tiny jingle bell in the center. Add sticker letters near the base. Use double-sided tape to adhere the cardstock to a 4½×6½-inch glitter paper and then to a folded 5×7-inch card.

Santa Ready

Felt, with its many colors and prints, is a fun fabric choice for holiday stockings. Large or small, these stocking designs can be personalized for all your favorite people. To make the stockings sturdier, line with iron-on interfacing.

TOPSY TURVY

Paisleys, turned every which way, create a playful pattern the entire family will love. Just choose their favorite colors in soft, easy-to-sew felt. Trace the patterns, page 156. Use the patterns to cut a stocking front and back and paisleys from felt. If desired, cut and iron on interfacing lining to stocking pieces as instructed by the manufacturer. For each outline, cut ¼-inch-wide strips from felt, piecing if needed. Thread a needle with embroidery floss. Use the photo as a guide for placing paisleys on stocking front; secure in place using running stitches. Outline each paisley with a thin felt strip, leaving a narrow border between felt pieces. When all paisleys and outlines are adhered to stocking front, use running stitches to embellish the stocking front, working stitches around the paisleys. Use running stitches to stitch the stocking front to the back; use pinking shears to trim the back piece slightly larger than the front. Add a felt loop for hanging.

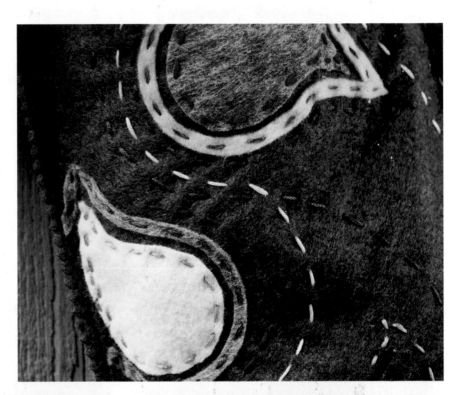

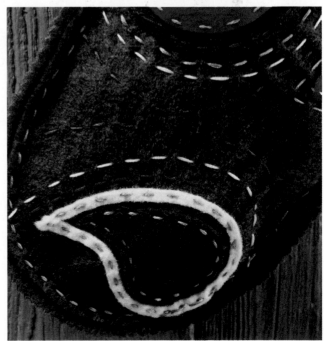

SIMPLY STATED

A stiffened felt snowflake is all it takes to decorate two mini stockings. Use them as treat holders or pair them for a larger wall presentation. For each stocking, trace the patterns, page 154. Use the patterns to cut a stocking front and back from felt. If desired, cut and iron on interfacing lining to stocking pieces as instructed by the manufacturer. Thread a needle with white embroidery floss; use it to tack half a snowflake on the stocking front, using the photo as a placement guide. Using contrasting running stitches, sew the stocking front to the back. Attach a felt loop for hanging.

FALLING FLAKES

A felt tablerunner provides ample motifs to make the whole crew stockings for Santa. Trace the stocking patterns, page 154. Use the patterns to cut a stocking front and back from felt. If desired, cut and iron on interfacing lining to stocking pieces as instructed by the manufacturer. Cut a section from felt snowflake tablerunner to fit stocking front. Thread a needle with white embroidery floss; tack snowflake runner to stocking. Stitch stocking front to back using matching embroidery floss and running stitches. Add a felt loop for hanging.

PATTERN PERFECT

Personalized stockings are so meaningful, as well as easy, using patterned felts and wide initialed cuffs. Trace the patterns, page 155. Use the patterns to cut a stocking front, back, cuff, and bow from felt. If desired, cut and iron on interfacing lining to stocking pieces as instructed by the manufacturer. For the initial, cut ¼-inch-wide strips from felt that contrast with cuff color, piecing if needed. Shape the strips into the desired letter on the cuff. Thread a needle with embroidery floss to stitch the initial in place. Align the cuff and stocking front on the back; stitch together and add a hanging loop.

CUTE CUFF

Felt strips, woven in a basket weave pattern, get permanent placement with extra-large cross-stitches holding the weave in place. Trace the patterns, page 157. Use the patterns to cut a stocking front, back, and cuff strips. If desired, cut and iron on interfacing lining to stocking pieces as instructed by the manufacturer. With points facing down, weave strips together; pin in place. Thread a needle with embroidery floss and stitch a large X in the center of each square. Stitch the stocking front to back; add a hanging loop.

Out with the Old

Ring in the new year with all things golden. Party guests will applaud your artistic uses for simple materials like glue and paper.

BALL DROP

These spheres are too pretty to wait until midnight to reveal. Hide glue transforms simple white yarn into iridescent gold to make New Year's globes that are most certainly dressed for the occasion.

WHAT YOU NEED
Balloon
White yarn
Scissors
Binder clip
2 bowls
Hide glue
Plastic spoon
Thin gold ribbon
Wide patterned ribbon with gold accents

WHAT YOU DO
1. Cover the work surface. Blow up balloon; tie off end.
2. Tie a 2-foot piece of yarn to a binder clip; set aside.

3. Put the balloon into a bowl to keep it from rolling. Put a 36-inch length of yarn into the second bowl as shown in Photo A.
4. Pour some hide glue over the yarn as shown in Photo B. Stir the yarn into the glue until covered, adding more glue if needed.
5. Pull the yarn between two fingers to remove excess glue. Wind the yarn around the balloon in a random fashion as shown in Photo C, crossing fibers as shown.
6. Continue wrapping pieces of glue-covered yarn around balloon until the desired look is achieved.
7. Attach the binder clip to the top of the balloon; hang to dry as shown in Photo D (an upper kitchen cabinet knob does the job).
8. When the glue is completely dry, the yarn will be very firm. Pop the balloon and remove it through one of the larger spaces.
9. Tie a narrow ribbon to the sphere for hanging. Use the wider ribbon to top off the decoration.

MERRY GOES 'ROUND

Clear glass candleholders get celebration ready with bands of gold wrapped around the surface. Soak a 36-inch-long strand of white yarn with golden hide glue; pull between fingers to remove excess glue. Start at the top and wrap three times, then wrap diagonally around the base ending with two wraps at the bottom; cut off extra yarn. Immediately wipe off any smeared glue from the glass using a cotton swab or folded paper towel dampened in hot water. Let the glue dry.

Never leave burning candles unattended.

A WAY WITH WORDS

Treat New Year's guests to some good vibes for the coming year. Cut strips of white paper, approximately ¾×4 inches; notch one end of each strip. Use a gold marking pen to write a positive wish on each paper banner. For each cracker, cut a 4-inch square from white cardstock. Roll paper into a tube; tape to secure. Cut a 5×8-inch piece of gold wrapping paper. Place the wrapping paper around the tube; tape. Pinch one end of wrapping paper, just beyond the paper tube; tie with ribbon. Place the fortune and a piece or two of candy, if desired, into the tube. Pinch the paper on the remaining end and tie with ribbon. Add a rhinestone initial for each party guest.

Drawer Decor

PICTORIAL

Make a scene—a wall-mounted wonderland—to enjoy all winter long. Use picture hangers to hang drawers on the wall. Fill the cubbies with holiday items and use the tops as shelves. The rustic display changes easily from season to season.

SERVICE WITH STYLE

A drawer, bread basket size, makes a sturdy serving piece. Grace a clean drawer with a cloth napkin before using it for food.

UPLIFTED

Make a sensational arrangement nesting real or faux blooms, berries, and greens in an elevated sewing machine drawer. To make each leg, use wood glue to join the open ends of two dowel caps together; let dry. Stain the legs to match the sewing machine drawer; let dry. Use wood glue to attach the legs the drawer. Line the drawer with short plastic liners or drinking glasses. Fill the containers halfway with water if using real flowers. Place greens around the edges and tuck in flowers at one end. Accent the opposite end with ornaments and berries.

SACRED SETTING

In lieu of a stable, pair drawers to house nativity figures. Once the figures are arranged, tuck in bottlebrush trees to fill in the gaps.

AS IS

Land greeting cards in a place of honor. A drawer offers plenty of room to display an array of cards. Sprigs of evergreen soften the edges.

**OVEN-ROASTED
BRUSSELS SPROUTS
WITH APPLES,
CHERRIES, AND
PECANS**
Recipe on page 108

food

This festive time of year brings busy days with gatherings both large and small. Here you'll find delicious recipes that make the season special.

BENNE PULL-APART ROLLS
Recipe on page 105

Love Me Tender

The reward of braising—roasting with liquid—is tender meat, poultry, or veggies with wonderful deep flavor.

BRAISED VEGETABLES AND CARAMELIZED LEEKS
Recipe on page 92

**COCONUT-CURRY
SHORT RIBS**
Recipe on page 92

BRAISED VEGETABLES AND CARAMELIZED LEEKS

PREP 15 minutes
COOK 20 minutes
BAKE 45 minutes at 325°F

WHAT YOU NEED

3   Tbsp. olive oil
3   cups thinly sliced leeks, turnips, rutabaga, or kohlrabi
1   tsp. salt
2½   cups reduced-sodium vegetable or chicken broth
6   stalks celery, trimmed to fit pan, strings removed*
1   lb. carrots, peeled or scrubbed, cut in half lengthwise if thick
1   lb. parsnips, peeled or scrubbed, cut in half lengthwise if thick
5   Tbsp. butter
1   lemon (2 tsp. zest, 3 Tbsp. juice)
3   sprigs fresh thyme
1   bay leaf
⅓   cup panko
3   Tbsp. chopped almonds
1   Tbsp. minced garlic
¼   cup chopped fresh parsley

WHAT YOU DO

1. Preheat oven to 325°F. In a deep oven-going skillet or 5-qt. Dutch oven heat 2 Tbsp. oil over medium-low heat. Stir in leeks and ½ tsp. salt. Cover; cook 6 to 8 minutes or until leeks are tender but not browned. Uncover; stir in 1 Tbsp. broth. Cook 20 to 25 minutes or until caramelized and starting to break into small bits, stirring in 1 Tbsp. broth every 6 to 8 minutes (¼ cup total).
2. Stir in remaining 2¼ cups broth, the celery, carrots, parsnips, butter, lemon juice, thyme, and bay leaf. Bring to a simmer, scraping pan to loosen browned bits. Cover; transfer to oven. Bake 45 to 55 minutes or until vegetables are fork-tender.
3. Meanwhile, heat a small skillet over medium heat. Add panko, almonds, garlic, and remaining 1 Tbsp oil; cook and stir 2 to 3 minutes or until toasted. Remove from heat. Stir in parsley and lemon zest.
4. Transfer vegetables to a platter. Discard thyme and bay leaf. Pour braising liquid over vegetables. Top with panko mixture and remaining ½ tsp. salt. Makes 4 servings.
*Tip Remove strings from celery by peeling off ridges of the outer layer using a vegetable peeler.

COCONUT-CURRY SHORT RIBS

PREP 30 minutes
COOK 5 minutes
BAKE 2 hours at 325°F

WHAT YOU NEED

3   lb. bone-in beef short ribs, cut into 2- to 3-rib portions*
½   tsp. salt
1   Tbsp. coconut oil or vegetable oil
1   shallot, finely chopped
1   Tbsp. grated fresh ginger
2   tsp. minced fresh lemongrass
2   cloves garlic, minced
3   Tbsp. Thai red curry paste
1   Tbsp. packed brown sugar
1   14-oz. can unsweetened coconut milk
1   Tbsp. fish sauce
4   heads baby bok choy, halved lengthwise
     Mint leaves
     Lime wedges

WHAT YOU DO

1. Season meat with ½ tsp. salt. Preheat oven to 325°F. In a 5- to 6-qt. Dutch oven heat oil over medium-high heat. Cook ribs in batches 3 to 5 minutes on each side until deep brown. Transfer to plate.
2. Reduce heat to medium. Add shallot, ginger, lemongrass, and garlic; cook 1 minute. Stir in curry paste and brown sugar; cook 1 minute. Stir in coconut milk and fish sauce; bring to a simmer. Return ribs and juices to pot, meat side down. Cover; transfer to oven. Bake 2 to 2½ hours or until meat is fork-tender.
3. Transfer meat to a platter; keep warm. Skim fat from braising liquid. Bring liquid to a simmer over medium-high heat. Add bok choy; simmer 2 to 3 minutes or until just tender, turning once. Transfer bok choy to platter with meat. Pour braising liquid over. Serve with mint and lime wedges. Makes 4 servings.
*Tip Ask your butcher to cut the two- to three-rib portions for their pretty presentation. Single-rib portions are commonly found in the meat case and will also work in this recipe.

MOROCCAN TAGINE-STYLE CHICKEN THIGHS

PREP 20 minutes
ROAST 1 hour at 350°F

WHAT YOU NEED

4   tsp. ground cinnamon
1½   tsp. caraway seeds, crushed
1½   tsp. ground cumin
1½   tsp. ground cardamom
⅛   to ¼ tsp. cayenne pepper
8   cloves garlic, minced
12   chicken thighs, skinned (4 to 5 lb. total)
2   Tbsp. olive oil
1   14.5-oz. can reduced-sodium chicken broth
1   cup dried apricots, quartered
1   cup pitted dates, quartered
¼   cup sliced almonds, ground
1   tsp. ground turmeric
¾   tsp. salt
¼   tsp. black pepper
¼   tsp. saffron threads, crushed
⅓   cup snipped fresh cilantro
2   Tbsp. sliced almonds, toasted*
     Hot cooked couscous or rice (optional)

WHAT YOU NEED

1. Preheat oven to 350°F. In a bowl combine cinnamon, caraway seeds, cumin, cardamom, cayenne pepper, and garlic. Sprinkle spice mixture over chicken and rub in with your fingers.
2. In a 6- to 8-qt. pot or Dutch oven heat oil over medium-high heat. Brown chicken, half at a time, in hot oil 6 minutes, turning once. Add broth, apricots, dates, almonds, turmeric, salt, black pepper, and saffron. Roast 1 hour or until chicken is done (170°F) and tender.
3. Use a slotted spoon to transfer chicken mixture to a shallow serving dish. Sprinkle chicken with cilantro and sliced almonds. Skim fat from cooking liquid. Serve chicken with cooking liquid and, if desired, couscous. Makes 6 servings.
Slow Cooker Prepare as directed, except place chicken in a 6- to 7-qt. slow cooker. In a medium bowl combine broth, apricots, dates, ground almonds, turmeric, salt, pepper, and saffron; pour over chicken. Cover and cook on low 8 hours or high 4 hours.
*Tip Toast small amounts of nuts in a dry skillet 3 to 5 minutes until light brown, stirring frequently.

ZA'ATAR
CHICKEN AND
LENTILS

ZA'ATAR CHICKEN AND LENTILS

PREP 10 minutes
COOK 10 minutes
BAKE 45 minutes at 325°F

WHAT YOU NEED

6   bone-in, skin-on chicken thighs, excess fat trimmed
3   Tbsp. za'atar
2   Tbsp. olive oil
1   cup coarsely chopped onion
1   cup bite-size pieces carrot
2   cloves garlic, minced
3½ cups reduced-sodium chicken broth
1   cup French green lentils*
2   Tbsp. tomato paste
1   cup pitted green olives, such as Castelvetrano, whole or halved
    Lemon zest
    Fresh thyme sprigs

WHAT YOU DO

1. Preheat oven to 325°F. Season chicken with za'atar. In a deep oven-going skillet or 5-qt. Dutch oven heat oil over medium-high heat. Add chicken; cook 3 to 4 minutes on each side or until brown. Transfer to a plate.
2. Reduce heat to medium. Add onion and carrots to pot. Cook 4 to 5 minutes or until lightly browned. Stir in garlic; cook 1 minute. Stir in broth, lentils, and tomato paste. Return chicken and juices to pot. Bring to a simmer. Cover; transfer to oven. Bake 45 to 55 minutes or until chicken is done (175°F).
3. Transfer chicken to a platter; keep warm. Strain remaining mixture, reserving liquid. Add lentils and vegetables to chicken on platter; cover. Return liquid to pot. Boil over medium-high heat 10 to 15 minutes or until reduced by half. Pour cooking liquid over chicken and lentils. Top with olives, lemon zest, and thyme. Makes 6 servings.
*Tip French green lentils have a firm texture that holds up to longer cooking methods better than most other varieties.

DIJON BEEF AND
MUSHROOMS

CHIPOTLE PORK TACOS

PREP 20 minutes
COOK 15 minutes
BAKE 2 hours at 325°F

WHAT YOU NEED

2   to 2½ lb. boneless pork shoulder,
    trimmed and cut into 2-inch pieces
1   tsp. salt
2   Tbsp. vegetable oil
1   orange, cut into 6 wedges
1   cup sliced onion
2   cloves garlic, minced
1   tsp. ground cumin
1   tsp. dried oregano, crushed
1   12-oz. bottle dark lager beer or
    1½ cups beef broth
¾   cup orange juice
2   to 3 canned chipotle peppers in
    adobo sauce, finely chopped, plus
    1 Tbsp. adobo sauce
24 6-inch corn tortillas, warmed
2   cups finely shredded red cabbage
¾   cup crumbled queso fresco or feta
    cheese
    Cilantro (optional)

WHAT YOU NEED

1. Preheat oven to 325°F. Season meat
with salt. In a 5- to 6-qt. Dutch oven heat
1 Tbsp. oil over medium-high heat. Cook
meat in batches 3 to 5 minutes on each
side or until deep brown. Transfer to
a plate.
2. Reduce heat to medium. Add remaining
1 Tbsp. oil. Place orange wedges, cut sides
down, in pot; cook 2 minutes on each side
or until deep brown. Remove from pot; set
aside. Add onion to pot. Cook 3 minutes or
until lightly browned. Stir in garlic, cumin,
and oregano; cook 1 minute. Add beer,
orange juice, and chipotle peppers and
adobo sauce. Bring to a simmer, scraping
pan bottom. Return meat and juices to
pot; return to a simmer. Cover; transfer to
oven. Bake 2 to 2½ hours or until meat is
fork-tender.
3. Shred meat in pot. If there's too much
liquid, simmer over medium heat to slightly
thicken. Serve in doubled tortillas with
cabbage and cheese and, if desired,
sprinkle with cilantro. Serve with seared
orange wedges. Makes 6 servings.

DIJON BEEF AND
MUSHROOMS

PREP 30 minutes
BAKE 1 hour 30 minutes at 350°F

WHAT YOU NEED

2   to 3 Tbsp. vegetable oil
2   8-oz. pkg. button and/or cremini
    mushrooms, quartered
1   cup chopped onion
3   cloves garlic, minced
1½ lb. boneless beef sirloin steak, cut
    into 1-inch pieces
½   tsp. salt
¼   tsp. black pepper
⅔   cup reduced-sodium beef broth
⅔   cup dry white wine
3   Tbsp. Dijon mustard
1   Tbsp. snipped fresh thyme or 1 tsp.
    dried thyme, crushed
2   Tbsp. butter, softened
2   Tbsp. all-purpose flour
    Garlic toasts or hot cooked pasta
    (optional)

WHAT YOU DO

1. Preheat oven to 350°F. In an oven-
safe 5- to 6-qt. pot heat 1 Tbsp. oil over
medium-high heat. Add mushrooms,
onion, and garlic; cook and stir 6 minutes
or until tender and beginning to brown.
Remove mushroom mixture from pot.
2. Sprinkle meat with salt and pepper. In
the same pot heat 1 Tbsp. oil over medium-
high heat. Add half of the meat; cook until
just browned, 2 to 3 minutes. Transfer to a
bowl. Repeat with remaining meat, adding
more oil if necessary. Return all the meat
and the mushroom mixture to pot. Add
broth, wine, mustard, and dried thyme (if
using). Bring to boiling, stirring to combine.
Cover and pot and place in oven.
3. Bake 1 hour. In a small bowl stir together
butter and flour. Stir butter mixture and
fresh thyme (if using) into meat mixture in
pot. Bake, covered, 30 minutes more or
until meat is tender and sauce is slightly
thickened. Serve with garlic toasts or pasta
and, if desired, fresh thyme sprigs. Makes
4 servings.

CHIPOTLE PORK
TACOS

PULL-APARTS

These luscious and gooey pull-apart loaves are messy by nature.
Serve with plenty of napkins!

**SAUSAGE-PESTO
PULL-APART BREAD**

SAUSAGE-PESTO PULL-APART BREAD

PREP 25 minutes
BAKE 45 minutes at 350°F
RISE 1 hour 15 minutes
COOL 10 minutes

WHAT YOU NEED

- ¾ cup milk
- 1 pkg. active dry yeast
- 1 egg, lightly beaten
- ¼ cup butter, melted
- 1 Tbsp. granulated sugar
- ½ tsp. salt
- 3 cups all-purpose flour
- ⅓ cup + 1 Tbsp. basil pesto
- 8 oz. Italian sausage, cooked, drained, and crumbled
- ½ cup chopped roasted red sweet peppers
- 1½ cups shredded mozzarella cheese (6 oz.)
- 1 Tbsp. olive oil

WHAT YOU DO

1. In a small saucepan heat milk just until warm (105°F to 115°F). In a large bowl combine warm milk and yeast; stir until yeast is dissolved. Let stand 5 minutes.
2. Add egg, the ¼ cup melted butter, sugar, and salt to the yeast mixture. Beat with a mixer on medium until combined. Add half the flour; beat on low 30 seconds, scraping bowl as needed. Beat 1 minute on medium. Stir in remaining flour. Shape dough into a ball (dough will not be smooth). Place dough in a greased bowl; turn once to grease surface. Cover and let rise in a warm place until nearly double in size (45 to 60 minutes).
3. Grease a 9×5-inch loaf pan. Turn dough out onto a lightly floured surface. Roll dough into a 20×12-inch rectangle. Stir together ⅓ cup pesto and the sausage; spread over dough. Sprinkle with red peppers and cheese. Cut rectangle in half lengthwise to make two 20×6-inch strips. Cut each strip crosswise into five 6×4-inch strips. Carefully make two stacks

of five strips each. Cut each stack into 4×2-inch pieces. Loosely stagger pieces in pan, cut sides up. Cover and let rise in a warm place until nearly double in size (30 minutes).

4. Preheat oven to 350°F. Bake 45 minutes or until golden brown and an instant-read thermometer inserted near the center registers 200°F. Cool in pan 10 minutes. Transfer to a serving plate. In a small bowl combine remaining pesto and oil. Drizzle over loaf. Makes 10 servings.

Make Ahead Prepare as directed through Step 2, except do not let dough rise. Cover bowl and refrigerate up to 24 hours. Let dough stand at room temperature 30 minutes before continuing with Step 3.

PUMPKIN PULL-APART LOAF

PREP 30 minutes
RISE 1 hour 30 minutes
BAKE 35 minutes at 350°F
COOL 30 minutes

WHAT YOU NEED
¾   cup milk
1   pkg. active dry yeast
1   cup canned pumpkin
3   Tbsp. butter, melted
2   Tbsp. granulated sugar
1   egg yolk
1   tsp. salt
3   cups all-purpose flour
3   Tbsp. butter, melted
¾   cup packed brown sugar
1   Tbsp. ground cinnamon
1   recipe Cinnamon Glaze
    Chopped toasted pecans (optional)

WHAT YOU DO
1. In a small saucepan heat milk just until warm (105°F to 115°F). In a large bowl combine warm milk and yeast; stir to dissolve yeast. Let stand 5 to 10 minutes or until foamy.

2. Add ½ cup of the pumpkin and the next four ingredients (through salt) to yeast mixture. Beat with a mixer on medium until combined. Add half of the flour; beat on low 30 seconds, scraping bowl as needed. Beat on medium 3 minutes. Stir in remaining flour. Shape into a ball (dough will not be smooth). Place dough in a greased bowl, turning once to grease surface. Cover and let rise in a warm place until nearly double in size (45 to 60 minutes).

PUMPKIN
PULL-APART
LOAF

3. Butter a 9×5-inch loaf pan. Turn dough out onto a lightly floured surface. Roll into a 20×12-inch rectangle. In a small bowl combine remaining ½ cup pumpkin and 3 Tbsp. melted butter; spread over dough. Combine brown sugar and cinnamon; sprinkle over pumpkin mixture. Cut dough crosswise into five 12×4-inch strips. Stack strips, then cut crosswise into six 4×2-inch pieces, leaving stacks intact. Loosely stagger pieces, cut sides up, in prepared pan. Cover and let rise in a warm place until nearly double in size (about 45 minutes).

4. Preheat oven to 350°F. Bake 35 minutes or until golden, covering loosely with foil the last 10 minutes if needed to prevent overbrowning. Cool in pan on a wire rack 10 minutes. Remove from pan. Drizzle with Cinnamon Glaze and, if desired, sprinkle with pecans. Cool 20 minutes more. Makes 12 servings.

Cinnamon Glaze In a small bowl stir together 1 cup powdered sugar, 1 Tbsp. milk, and ½ tsp. each ground cinnamon and vanilla. If needed, stir in additional milk, 1 tsp. at a time, to reach drizzling consistency.

PULL-APART
PRETZEL
SKILLET

PULL-APART PRETZEL SKILLET

PREP 35 minutes
RISE 1 hour
BAKE 20 minutes at 400°F

WHAT YOU NEED

1   pkg. active dry yeast
½   tsp. sugar
¾   cup warm water
1½ cups all-purpose flour
1   cup whole wheat flour or all-purpose flour
1   tsp. salt
3   Tbsp. honey
2   tsp. vegetable oil
    Nonstick cooking spray
2   cups hot water
¼   cup baking soda
    Pretzel or kosher salt
1   8-oz. pkg. cream cheese, softened
1   cup wheat beer or lager
8   oz. mild cheddar cheese, shredded (2 cups)
8   oz. mozzarella cheese, shredded (2 cups)
1   tsp. garlic powder
¼   tsp. salt
    Snipped fresh rosemary (optional)

WHAT YOU DO

1. In a small saucepan heat water just until warm (105°F to 115°F). In a small bowl dissolve yeast and sugar in ¾ cup warm water. Let stand 5 minutes or until foamy.
2. In a large bowl combine both flours and 1 tsp. salt. Make a well in center and add honey, oil, and yeast mixture. Stir until dough starts to come together. Transfer dough to a lightly floured surface and knead until smooth, 7 to 8 minutes.
3. Lightly coat a large bowl with nonstick cooking spray. Transfer dough to prepared bowl. Turn dough to coat. Cover and let rise until double in size (about 1 hour).
4. Preheat oven to 400°F. In a medium bowl combine 2 cups hot water and baking soda. Divide dough into 16 pieces. Roll each piece into a ball and dip into the baking soda-water mixture. Arrange dough balls around edge of a 12-inch cast-iron skillet, leaving the center open. Score the top of each dough ball with an "x". Sprinkle balls with pretzel salt.
5. In a medium bowl beat cream cheese with a mixer on medium to high 30 seconds or until smooth. Beat in beer until combined (mixture will not be smooth). Stir in cheddar cheese, mozzarella cheese, garlic powder, and ¼ tsp. salt. Spoon cheese mixture into center of skillet. Bake 20 minutes or until pretzels are browned and cheese is melted. Serve immediately. If desired, sprinkle with snipped rosemary. Makes 16 servings.

MAPLE-MOCHA PULL-APART BREAD WITH ALMONDS

PREP 45 minutes
RISE 1 hour 30 minutes
COOL 10 minutes
BAKE 40 minutes at 350°F
COOL 35 minutes

WHAT YOU NEED

- 4 to 4½ cups all-purpose flour
- ¼ cup unsweetened cocoa powder
- 1 pkg. active dry yeast
- 1½ cups milk
- ¼ cup butter, cut up
- ¼ cup pure maple syrup
- 1 Tbsp. instant espresso coffee powder
- 1 tsp. salt
- 1 egg
- 1 cup heavy cream
- 1 Tbsp. butter
- ¾ cup pure maple syrup
- 1½ cups powdered sugar
- 1 to 2 Tbsp. milk
- ⅓ cup granulated sugar
- ½ tsp. ground cinnamon
- ⅔ cup sliced almonds, lightly toasted (tip, page 114)

WHAT YOU DO

1. In a large bowl combine 2 cups of the flour, the cocoa powder, and yeast; set aside. In a medium saucepan heat and whisk together the next five ingredients (through salt) just until warm (120°F to 130°F) and butter almost melts. Add milk mixture to flour mixture; add egg. Beat with a mixer on low 30 seconds, scraping bowl frequently. Beat on high 3 minutes. Stir in as much of the remaining flour as you can.

2. Turn dough out onto a lightly floured surface. Knead in enough of the remaining flour to make a soft dough that is smooth and elastic (3 to 5 minutes total). Shape dough into a ball. Place in a lightly greased bowl; turn to grease surface of dough. Cover; let rise in a warm place until double in size (about 1 hour).

3. While dough is rising, in a medium saucepan bring heavy cream to boiling; reduce heat. Boil gently, uncovered, 12 to 14 minutes or until reduced to ½ cup, stirring occasionally. Stir in 1 Tbsp. butter. Cool 10 minutes. Gradually whisk in ¾ cup maple syrup. For icing, remove 3 Tbsp. of the syrup mixture to a small bowl; stir in powdered sugar and enough milk to make a thick drizzling consistency; cover and set aside.

4. Punch dough down. Turn out onto a lightly floured surface. Divide into quarters. Cover and let rest 10 minutes. Meanwhile, in a small bowl combine granulated sugar and cinnamon. Generously grease a 10-inch fluted tube pan.

5. Roll each piece of dough into a rope about 20 inches long. Cut ropes into 1-inch pieces. Roll each piece in sugar-cinnamon mixture. Spoon half the remaining cooled syrup mixture into the bottom of prepared pan. Sprinkle with almonds. Arrange half the dough pieces on almonds. Sprinkle with half of the remaining sugar-cinnamon mixture. Drizzle remaining syrup mixture over dough in pan. Arrange remaining dough in the pan. Sprinkle with remaining sugar-cinnamon mixture. Cover and let rise in a warm place until nearly double in size (30 to 45 minutes).

6. Preheat oven to 350°F. Bake 40 to 45 minutes (internal temperature should be 190°F to 200°F). Cool in pan 5 minutes. Loosen sides and center with a thin metal spatula or table knife. Invert onto a serving platter. Spoon any syrup and nuts that remain in pan over bread. Cool 30 minutes. Drizzle with the maple icing before serving. Makes 16 servings.

Make Ahead After assembling pull-apart bread in pan, cover with plastic wrap and chill 8 to 24 hours. Before baking, remove pan from refrigerator and let stand, covered, 1½ hours. Discard plastic wrap and bake at 350°F 45 minutes.

MAPLE-MOCHA
PULL-APART BREAD
WITH ALMONDS

BENNE
PULL-APART
ROLLS

BENNE PULL-APART ROLLS

PREP 40 minutes
RISE 1 hour 30 minutes
REST 10 minutes
BAKE 15 minutes at 375°F

WHAT YOU NEED
1   cup whole milk
⅓   cup sugar
2   pkg. active dry yeast (4½ tsp.)
¼   cup unsalted butter, softened
1½   tsp. salt
3   eggs
3¾   cups all-purpose flour
2   Tbsp. benne (white sesame) seeds
1   Tbsp. black sesame seeds
2   Tbsp. chopped fresh herbs or whole herb sprigs, such as oregano, thyme, rosemary, and/or sage

WHAT YOU DO
1. In a small saucepan heat milk and sugar over medium heat until just warm (105°F to 115°F). Pour into a large bowl. Stir in yeast and let stand 5 minutes or until foamy.
2. Add butter, salt, two of the eggs, and 1 cup flour to milk mixture. Beat with a mixer on low until smooth. Beat in as much remaining flour as you can. Stir in as much remaining flour as you can.
3. Transfer dough to a lightly floured surface. Knead in remaining flour until dough is soft and smooth, but still a little sticky, about 4 minutes. Butter a large bowl; add dough to bowl, turning once to grease surface. Cover and let rise until double in size (about 1 hour).
4. Line a large baking sheet with parchment paper. Using a 12-inch plate as guide, draw a circle on the paper. Turn paper over.
5. Punch dough down. Turn out onto the floured surface. Cover and let rest 10 minutes. Divide dough into six even pieces. Pinch off six pieces from each dough piece, shaping each into a ball (36 total balls). Arrange 20 balls about ½ inch apart on the circle on the paper. Arrange 16 balls about 1 inch inside the first ring of dough balls (these balls will touch). Cover loosely with a towel and let rise until dough is nearly doubled (about 30 minutes).
6. Preheat oven to 375°F. Beat remaining egg with 1 Tbsp. water. Gently brush tops of dough balls with egg mixture; sprinkle with

seeds. Bake 15 to 18 minutes or until golden brown. Top with herb sprigs. Serve warm or room temperature. Makes 18 servings.
Make Ahead Bake and cool wreath as directed. Wrap in heavy foil. Freeze up to 1 month. To reheat, place frozen wrapped rolls in a 350°F oven 15 minutes or until warm.

BANANA PRALINE CRUNCH PULL-APART BREAD

PREP 25 minutes
RISE 1 hour 25 minutes
BAKE 45 minutes at 350°F
COOL 30 minutes

WHAT YOU NEED
¾   cup milk
1   pkg. active dry yeast
1   egg, lightly beaten
¼   cup butter, melted
2   Tbsp. granulated sugar
½   tsp. salt
3   cups all-purpose flour
¼   cup butter, melted
1½   cups finely chopped bananas
¾   cup packed brown sugar
½   cup chopped, toasted pecans
1   tsp. ground cinnamon
1   recipe Coconut-Pecan Topping
2   oz. semisweet chocolate, melted

WHAT YOU DO
1. In a small saucepan heat milk just until warm (105°F to 115°F). In a large bowl combine warm milk and yeast; stir until yeast is dissolved. Let stand 5 minutes.
2. Add egg, ¼ cup melted butter, sugar, and salt to the yeast mixture. Beat with a mixer on medium until combined. Add half the flour; beat on low 30 seconds, scraping bowl as needed. Beat 1 minute on medium. Stir in remaining flour. Shape dough into a ball (dough will not be smooth). Place dough in a greased bowl; turn once to grease surface. Cover and let rise in a warm place until nearly double in size (45 to 60 minutes).
3. Grease a 9×5-inch loaf pan. Turn dough out onto a lightly floured surface. Roll dough into a 20×12-inch rectangle. Brush with ¼ cup melted butter. Sprinkle with bananas, brown sugar, pecans, and cinnamon. Cut rectangle in half lengthwise to make two 20×6-inch strips. Cut each strip crosswise into five 6×4-inch strips.

BANANA PRALINE CRUNCH PULL-APART BREAD

Carefully make two stacks of five strips each. Cut each stack into 4×2-inch pieces. Loosely stagger pieces in pan, cut sides up. Sprinkle with Coconut-Pecan Topping. Cover and let rise in a warm place until nearly double in size (40 to 45 minutes).
4. Preheat oven to 350°F. Bake 45 minutes or until golden brown (internal temperature should be 200°F). Cool in pan 10 minutes. Transfer to serving plate. Drizzle with melted chocolate. Cool 20 minutes. Makes 10 servings.
Coconut-Pecan Topping In a medium bowl combine ¼ cup all-purpose flour, ¼ cup packed brown sugar, and ¼ tsp. ground cinnamon. Cut in 2 Tbsp. butter until mixture resembles coarse crumbs. Stir in 2 Tbsp. flaked coconut and 2 Tbsp. chopped pecans.
Make Ahead Prepare as directed through Step 2, except do not let dough rise. Cover bowl and refrigerate up to 24 hours. Let dough stand at room temperature 30 minutes before continuing with Step 3.

SIDES & PIES

Enjoy these fresh takes on savory sides and irresistible pies, perfect for pairing with hearty mains.

CORN PUDDING CASSEROLE

CORN PUDDING CASSEROLE

PREP 30 minutes
BAKE 50 minutes at 350°F

WHAT YOU NEED

- 6 dried tomatoes (not oil-pack)
- ½ cup chopped onion
- 2 cloves garlic, minced
- 2 Tbsp. butter
- 1¼ cups shredded zucchini
- 1 16-oz. pkg. frozen whole kernel corn, thawed
- 6 eggs, lightly beaten
- 3 cups whole milk
- ¾ cup yellow cornmeal
- 1 15-oz. carton whole milk ricotta cheese
- 2 tsp. dried Italian seasoning, crushed
- 1 tsp. salt
- ¼ tsp. black pepper
- 1 cup finely shredded Parmesan cheese (4 oz.)
- 1 cup panko
- 1 Tbsp. butter, melted
  Fresh rosemary sprigs (optional)

WHAT YOU DO

1. Preheat oven to 350°F. Grease a 3-qt. baking dish; set aside. In a small bowl cover tomatoes with boiling water. Let stand 15 minutes; drain. Chop tomatoes; set aside.
2. Meanwhile, in a large skillet cook onion and garlic in 2 Tbsp. hot butter over medium heat 4 minutes or until tender. Add zucchini; cook 2 minutes more. Stir in corn and chopped tomatoes; set aside.
3. In a large bowl whisk together eggs and milk. Gradually whisk in cornmeal. Whisk in ricotta cheese, Italian seasoning, salt, and pepper. Stir in the corn mixture and Parmesan cheese. Carefully pour into prepared dish (dish will be full).
4. Bake 20 minutes. Meanwhile, in a bowl toss together panko and 1 Tbsp. melted butter. Sprinkle on top of casserole. Bake 30 minutes or until the top is brown and a knife inserted into the center comes out clean. If desired, top with zucchini and rosemary sprigs. Makes 12 servings.
Make Ahead Prepare as directed, except do not preheat oven and cool zucchini mixture to room temperature after Step 2. Once cool, continue with Step 3 and pour mixture into prepared baking dish. Cover tightly with foil; chill up to 24 hours. Stir corn mixture before baking. Bake and top as directed in Step 4.

ROASTED BEET SALAD WITH SHREDDED GREENS, GOLDEN RAISINS, AND PINE NUTS

ROASTED BEET SALAD WITH SHREDDED GREENS, GOLDEN RAISINS, AND PINE NUTS

PREP 10 minutes
COOK 15 minutes
ROAST 55 minutes at 450°F

WHAT YOU NEED

- 2 lb. beets with leafy tops
- 2 sprigs fresh rosemary
- 3 Tbsp. olive oil
- ¾ cup balsamic vinegar
  Salt
  Black pepper
- 1 cup crumbled ricotta salata or feta cheese (4 oz.)
- ⅓ cup golden raisins
- 2 Tbsp. pine nuts, toasted

WHAT YOU DO

1. Preheat oven to 450°F. Cut tops from beets; set aside. Place beets and rosemary on a large piece of heavy foil; drizzle with 1 Tbsp. oil. Bring up two opposite edges of foil; seal with a double fold. Fold in remaining ends to completely enclose, leaving space for steam to build. Roast 55 minutes or until tender. Carefully open packet to release steam. Cool until beets are easy to handle. Peel skins from beets and cut into wedges. Discard rosemary.
2. For balsamic reduction, pour vinegar into a small saucepan. Bring to boiling; reduce heat. Simmer, uncovered, 15 minutes or until reduced to ¼ cup. Cool (reduction will thicken as it cools).
3. Meanwhile, remove stems from beet tops; cut tops into fine shreds. In a large bowl gently toss warm roasted beets and beet tops with remaining 2 Tbsp. oil. Season to taste with salt and pepper.
4. Arrange beet mixture on a platter and sprinkle with ricotta salta, raisins, and pine nuts. Drizzle with balsamic reduction. Makes 4 servings.

OVEN-ROASTED BRUSSELS SPROUTS WITH APPLES, CHERRIES, AND PECANS

PREP 10 minutes
ROAST 20 minutes at 425°F

WHAT YOU NEED

1   lb. Brussels sprouts
2   Tbsp. olive oil
½   tsp. kosher salt
⅛   tsp. cayenne pepper
1   cup sliced or coarsely chopped apple
½   cup dried cherries or cranberries
¼   cup chopped pecans
¼   cup bottled red wine vinaigrette, or desired vinaigrette

WHAT YOU DO

1. Preheat oven to 425°F. Line a 15×10-inch baking pan with foil. Trim stems and remove any wilted outer leaves from Brussels sprouts. Halve sprouts lengthwise.
2. Place Brussels sprouts in the prepared pan. Drizzle with oil and sprinkle with salt and cayenne pepper; toss to combine.
3. Roast, uncovered, 15 minutes. Stir in apple, dried cherries, and pecans. Roast, uncovered, 5 to 10 minutes more or until sprouts are crisp-tender and lightly browned. Drizzle with vinaigrette; toss gently to coat. Makes 4 servings.

MALLOW-PRALINE SWEET POTATO PIE

PREP 45 minutes
BAKE 14 minutes at 450°F/ 45 minutes at 375°F
COOL 1 hour

WHAT YOU NEED

1   recipe Pastry for a Single-Crust Pie (recipe, page 111)
1⅔ cups cooked, mashed sweet potatoes* or one 17.2-oz. can whole sweet potatoes, drained and mashed
⅓   cup granulated sugar
¼   cup pure maple syrup
1   tsp. finely chopped crystallized ginger or ½ tsp. ground ginger
½   tsp. ground cinnamon
½   tsp. freshly grated nutmeg or ¼ teaspoon ground nutmeg
¼   tsp. ground allspice
⅛   tsp. salt
3   eggs, lightly beaten
1   cup buttermilk or sour milk**
2   Tbsp. butter
2   Tbsp. packed brown sugar
2   Tbsp. pure maple syrup
1   Tbsp. milk
½   cup chopped pecans
1   cup tiny marshmallows

WHAT YOU DO

1. Preheat oven to 450°F. Prepare Pastry for a Single-Crust Pie. On a lightly floured surface, use your hands to slightly flatten pastry. Roll pastry from center to edges into a circle about 12 inches in diameter. Wrap pastry circle around the rolling pin. Unroll into a 9-inch pie plate. Ease pastry into pie plate without stretching it. Trim pastry to ½ inch beyond edge of pie plate. Fold under extra pastry even with the plate's edge. Crimp edge as desired. Generously prick bottom and sides of pastry with a fork.

OVEN-ROASTED BRUSSELS SPROUTS WITH APPLES, CHERRIES, AND PECANS

**MALLOW-PRALINE
SWEET POTATO PIE**

Line pastry with a double thickness of foil. Bake 8 minutes; remove foil. Bake 6 or until golden. Cool on a wire rack.

2. Reduce oven temperature to 375°F. For filling, in a large bowl stir together sweet potatoes, granulated sugar, ¼ cup maple syrup, ginger, cinnamon, nutmeg, allspice, and salt. Add eggs; beat lightly with a fork just until combined. Gradually stir in buttermilk until thoroughly combined.

3. Place baked pastry shell on a foil-lined baking sheet on the oven rack. Carefully pour filling into pastry shell. Bake 30 minutes.

4. Meanwhile, in a small saucepan melt butter over medium heat. Gradually stir in brown sugar, 2 Tbsp. maple syrup, and milk. Cook and stir until mixture comes to boiling. With pie on oven rack, sprinkle partially baked pie with pecans and marshmallows. Carefully pour hot brown sugar mixture over the top. Bake 15 to 20 minutes more or until center appears set when shaken. Cool on a wire rack at least 1 hour. Cover and chill within 2 hours. Makes 8 servings.

*Tip To prepare mashed sweet potatoes, in a covered medium saucepan cook about 18 oz. peeled, cubed sweet potatoes in enough boiling salted water to cover 25 to 30 minutes or until tender. Drain potatoes. Mash potatoes with a potato masher or beat with a mixer on low just until light and fluffy.

**Tip To make 1 cup sour milk, place 1 Tbsp. lemon juice or vinegar in a glass measuring cup. Add milk to equal 1 cup; stir. Let stand 5 minutes before using.

MAPLE, APPLE,
AND CHEDDAR PIE

MAPLE, APPLE, AND CHEDDAR PIE

PREP 30 minutes
BAKE 1 hour at 375°F
COOL 1 hour

WHAT YOU NEED
1   recipe Pastry for Double-Crust Pie
½   cup sugar
2   Tbsp. all-purpose flour
½   tsp. ground cinnamon
¼   tsp. salt

5   cups thinly sliced, peeled tart apples (5 medium)
1½ cups shredded white cheddar cheese (6 oz.)
¼   cup maple syrup
1   Tbsp. heavy cream
1   egg, beaten
1   Tbsp. water, milk, or cream
     Sugar
2   Tbsp. maple syrup
¼   cup chopped pecans, toasted (tip, page 114) (optional)

WHAT YOU DO
1. Preheat oven to 375°F. Prepare Pastry for Double-Crust Pie. On a lightly floured surface, use your hands to slightly flatten one pastry ball. Roll pastry into a 12-inch circle. Line a 9-inch pie plate with pastry circle.
2. For filling, in a large bowl stir together ½ cup sugar, flour, cinnamon, and salt. Add apples; toss gently to coat. Add cheese and the ¼ cup maple syrup; toss gently to combine. Transfer filling to the pastry-lined pie plate. Drizzle with cream. Trim bottom

pastry to edge of pie plate. Use a 1- to 1½-inch cutter to cut holly leaf shapes from dough scraps. Roll out remaining pastry into a 12-inch circle and cut into ½-inch strips (or cut varying widths). Arrange half the strips going one direction; turn pie 90 degrees. Add remaining strips. Place holly leaf shapes on some of the strips. In a small bowl, whisk together egg and water until combined. Brush strips and holly leaves with some of the egg wash. Lightly sprinkle leaves with sugar.

3. To prevent overbrowning, cover edge of pie with foil. Bake 40 minutes; remove foil. Bake 20 minutes more or until apples are tender and pastry is golden brown. Transfer to a wire rack. Brush pie with the 2 Tbsp. maple syrup. If desired, sprinkle with pecans. Cool 1 hour. Serve slightly warm. Makes 8 servings.

Pastry for Double-Crust Pie In a large bowl stir together 2½ cups all-purpose flour and 1 tsp. salt. Using a pastry blender, cut in ½ cup shortening and ¼ cup butter, cut up, or shortening until pea size. Sprinkle 1 Tbsp. ice water over part of the flour mixture; toss gently with a fork. Push moistened pastry to side of bowl. Repeat moistening flour mixture, gradually adding ice water (½ to ⅔ cup total) until mixture begins to come together. Gather pastry into a ball, kneading gently just until it holds together. Divide into two portions; form two balls.

CHOCOLATE MIXED NUT PIE

PREP 25 minutes
BAKE 45 minutes at 350°F

WHAT YOU NEED

1   recipe Pastry for Single-Crust Pie
3   eggs, lightly beaten
1   cup light-color corn syrup
⅔   cup packed dark brown sugar
⅓   cup butter, melted
1   tsp. instant espresso coffee powder
1¼   cups dry-roasted salted mixed nuts, coarsely chopped
3   oz. sweet-style Mexican chocolate or bittersweet chocolate, chopped
1   recipe Cinnamon Whipped Cream or Cinnamon ice cream (optional)

WHAT YOU DO

1. Preheat oven to 350°F. Prepare pastry. On a lightly floured surface, slightly flatten pastry. Roll into a 12-inch circle. Transfer to a 9-inch pie plate, being careful not to stretch pastry. Trim to ½ inch beyond edge

CHOCOLATE
MIXED NUT PIE

of plate, fold pastry under even with rim, and crimp as desired.

2. In a medium bowl whisk together eggs, corn syrup, brown sugar, butter, and espresso powder until combined. Stir in nuts and chocolate.

3. Place pastry-lined pie plate on oven rack. Carefully pour filling into pastry shell. To prevent overbrowning, cover edge of pie with foil. Bake 25 minutes; remove foil. Bake 20 to 25 minutes more or until a knife inserted near center comes out clean. Cool on a wire rack. Cover; chill within 2 hours. Serve with cinnamon ice cream or Cinnamon Whipped Cream. Makes 8 servings.

Pastry for a Single-Crust Pie In a medium bowl stir together 1½ cups all-purpose flour and ¼ tsp. salt. Using a pastry blender, cut in ¼ cup shortening or lard and ¼ cup butter, cut up, until pea size. Sprinkle 1 Tbsp. ice water over part of the flour mixture; toss gently with a fork. Push moistened pastry to side of bowl. Repeat moistening flour mixture, gradually adding ice water (¼ to ⅓ cup total) until mixture begins to come together. Gather pastry into a ball, kneading gently just until it holds together.

Cinnamon Whipped Cream In a chilled small bowl beat ½ cup heavy cream, 1 Tbsp. sugar, 1½ tsp. coffee liqueur (optional), ¼ tsp. vanilla, and ⅛ tsp. cinnamon with a mixer on medium until soft peaks form (tips curl).

White Christmas

Keep the winter spirit close with a batch or two of these pristine white treats.

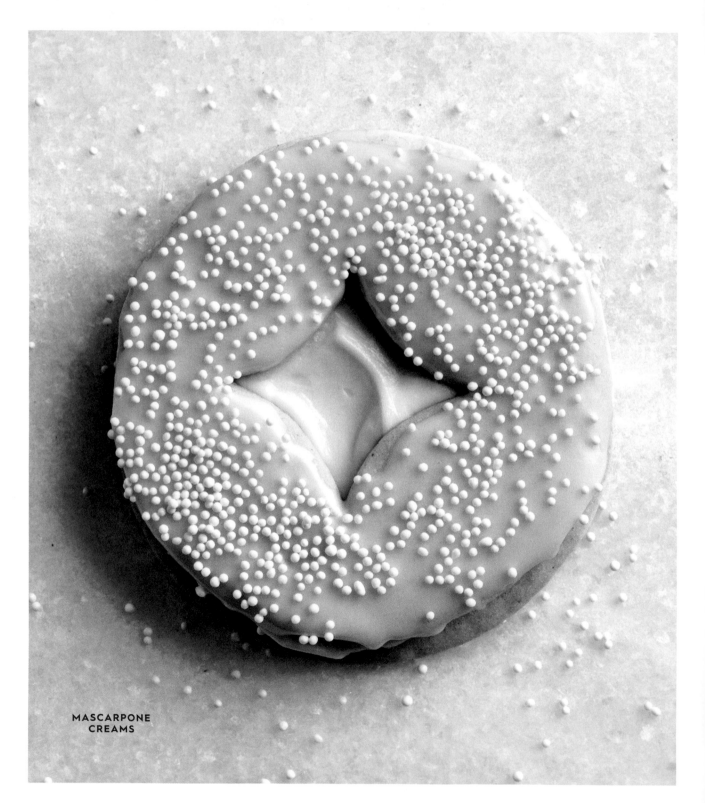

MASCARPONE
CREAMS

MASCARPONE CREAMS

PREP 45 minutes
BAKE 5 minutes per batch at 375°F
COOL 1 minute

WHAT YOU NEED
½   cup butter, softened
½   cup mascarpone cheese or ½ of an 8-oz. pkg. cream cheese, softened
1   cup granulated sugar
1   tsp. baking powder
¼   tsp. baking soda
¼   tsp. salt
¼   tsp. ground nutmeg
1   egg
2½   cups all-purpose flour
1   recipe Powdered Sugar Glaze
    White nonpareils (optional)
1   recipe Mascarpone Filling

WHAT YOU DO
1. In a large bowl beat butter and mascarpone cheese with a mixer on medium 30 seconds. Add the next five ingredients (through nutmeg) and beat until combined. Beat in egg. Beat in as much flour as you can; stir in any remaining flour. Divide dough in half. If needed, cover and chill 30 to 60 minutes or until dough is easy to handle.
2. Preheat oven to 375°F. On a lightly floured surface, roll one portion of dough at a time until ⅛ inch thick. Using a 3-inch round cookie cutter, cut out dough, rerolling scraps as needed. Using a 1-inch round cookie cutter, cut out centers from half of the cookies. Place 2 inches apart on an ungreased cookie sheet.
3. Bake 5 to 6 minutes or until edges are light brown. Cool on cookie sheet 1 minute. Remove; cool on a wire rack. Spread cookies with cutout centers with Powdered Sugar Glaze and, if desired, immediately sprinkle with nonpareils. Let stand until glaze is set.
4. Spread bottoms of whole cookies with Mascarpone Filling. Top with iced cookies, bottom sides down. Makes 16 sandwich cookies.
Powdered Sugar Glaze In a small bowl stir together 1¼ cups powdered sugar, 1 Tbsp. milk, and ½ tsp. vanilla. If needed, stir in additional milk, 1 tsp. at a time, to reach thin spreading consistency.
Mascarpone Filling In a large bowl beat ½ cup softened mascarpone or cream cheese with a mixer until fluffy. Beat in ½ tsp. vanilla. Gradually beat in 1½ cups powdered sugar until creamy.
2½-inch Sandwich Cookies Prepare as directed, except use a 2½-inch round cookie cutter to cut out dough. Use a ¾-inch round cookie cutter to cut out centers. Spread each whole cookie with 1½ to 2 tsp. filling. Makes about 28 (2½-inch) sandwich cookies.
To Store Layer cookies between waxed paper in an airtight container. Store in refrigerator up to 3 days or freeze up to 3 months.

ANGEL KISSES

PREP 25 minutes
BAKE 15 minutes per batch at 325°F

WHAT YOU NEED
4   egg whites
4   cups powdered sugar
2   cups chopped toasted pecans or candied pecans

WHAT YOU DO
1. Preheat oven to 325°F. Line a large cookie sheet with foil. Lightly grease foil.
2. In a large bowl beat egg whites with a mixer on high until soft peaks form (tips curl). Gradually add powdered sugar, about ¼ cup at a time, beating on medium just until combined. Beat on high until stiff peaks form (tips stand straight). Fold in nuts.
3. Drop mixture by teaspoons 2 inches apart onto prepared cookie sheet. Bake 15 minutes or until very light brown (cookies will puff and sides will split during baking). Remove; cool on a wire rack. Makes 36 cookies.
To Store Layer cookies between waxed paper in an airtight container. Store at room temperature up to 2 days or freeze up to 3 months.

ANGEL KISSES

WHITE CHOCOLATE-MACADAMIA BLONDIES

PREP 30 minutes
BAKE 30 minutes at 350°F

WHAT YOU NEED

    Nonstick cooking spray
½   cup butter
2   oz. white baking chocolate with
    cocoa butter, chopped
2   eggs
⅔   cup sugar
1   tsp. vanilla
1   cup all-purpose flour
½   tsp. baking powder
    Dash salt
1   cup chopped macadamia nuts or
    toasted pecans*
1   cup white baking chips
2   oz. white baking chocolate with
    cocoa butter, melted

WHAT YOU DO

1. Preheat oven to 350°F. Line an 8-inch square baking pan with foil, extending foil over edges. Coat foil with cooking spray.
2. In a medium saucepan cook and stir butter and 2 oz. chopped white chocolate over low heat until melted and smooth. Remove from heat. Add eggs, sugar, and vanilla. Beat lightly with a wooden spoon just until combined. In a small bowl stir together flour, baking powder, and salt. Stir flour mixture into white chocolate mixture just until combined. Stir in nuts and ½ cup of the white baking chips. Spread batter into prepared pan. Sprinkle with remaining ½ cup white baking chips.
3. Bake 30 to 35 minutes or until top is golden. Cool in pan on a wire rack. Use edges of foil to lift uncut bars out of the pan. Cut into bars. Drizzle with 2 oz. melted white chocolate; let stand until chocolate is set. Makes 16 bars.

*Tip To toast a larger amount of nuts, preheat oven to 350°F. Spread nuts in a shallow baking pan. Bake 5 to 10 minutes or until nuts are light brown, shaking pan once or twice.

To Store Place bars in a single layer in an airtight container. Store in refrigerator up to 2 days or freeze for up to 1 month.

IT TAKES ALL KINDS

White chocolate does not contain chocolate liqueur, but it does contain cocoa butter, which gives it a rich mouthfeel. Before you buy, know what you're looking for because these products don't all behave the same way.

WHITE CHOCOLATE BARS
If a recipe calls for white chocolate, this is what you want. (Check the ingredients list for cocoa butter.) It has a rich vanilla flavor with hints of chocolate. Watch closely when melting to prevent burning.

WHITE BAKING CHIPS
The word chocolate is missing here for a reason. These chips contain oil instead of cocoa butter as the fat. Their flavor and mouthfeel are different, but they work well stirred into bars, cookies, and other treats.

WHITE CANDY COATING
Like baking chips, candy coating (also known as almond bark) contains vegetable oils, milk, and sugar. It has no chocolate flavor, but it melts smoothly and coats evenly.

WHITE-CHOCOLATE-
MACADAMIA BLONDIES

WHITE CHOCOLATE,
COCONUT, AND
CASHEW FUDGE

WHITE CHOCOLATE, COCONUT, AND CASHEW FUDGE

PREP 20 minutes
CHILL 1 hour

WHAT YOU NEED

- Nonstick cooking spray
- 1 lb. good-quality white baking chocolate, chopped
- 1 14-oz. can sweetened condensed milk
- ¾ cup chopped salted cashews
- ½ cup chopped coconut, toasted*
- 1 tsp. vanilla
- ¼ tsp. coconut extract (optional)
- White sprinkles, jimmies, and/or shaved white baking chocolate
- Sea salt flakes

WHAT YOU DO

1. Line an 8- or 9-inch square baking pan with foil, extending foil over edges. Lightly coat foil with cooking spray.
2. In a medium heavy saucepan cook and stir chopped white chocolate and sweetened condensed milk over medium-low just until smooth. Remove from heat. Stir in cashews, coconut, vanilla, and, if desired, coconut extract.
3. Spread mixture in prepared pan. Top with sprinkles, jimmies, and/or shaved white chocolate and salt. Cover; chill 1 to 2 hours or until firm. Use foil to lift uncut fudge from pan. Cut into small squares. Makes 36 pieces.
*Tip To toast coconut, preheat oven to 350°F. Spread coconut in a foil-lined shallow baking pan. Bake 5 to 10 minutes or until golden, stirring once or twice.
To Store Layer fudge between waxed paper in an airtight container. Store in refrigerator up to 1 week or freeze up to 2 months.

PISTACHIO BALLS

PISTACHIO BALLS

PREP 30 minutes
BAKE 12 minutes per batch at 350°F

WHAT YOU NEED

- 1 cup butter, softened
- ¼ cup granulated sugar
- ¼ cup packed brown sugar
- ½ tsp. orange or lemon zest
- ¼ tsp. salt
- 2 tsp. vanilla
- 2 cups all-purpose flour
- 1 cup finely chopped pistachio nuts
- Powdered sugar

WHAT YOU DO

1. Preheat oven to 350°F. In a large bowl beat butter with a mixer on medium 30 seconds. Add both sugars, orange zest, and salt; beat until combined, scraping bowl as needed. Beat in vanilla. Beat in flour. Stir in pistachios.
2. Shape dough into 1-inch balls. Place 1 inch apart on an ungreased cookie sheet. Bake 12 minutes or just until bottoms begin to brown. Remove; cool on a wire rack. Toss cookies in powdered sugar to coat. Makes 66 cookies.

Make-It-Mine Linzer Cookies

Linzer cookies were adapted from the linzertorte—a traditional holiday tart originating in the Austrian city of Linz. With a peek-a-boo window of jam inside, they are the focal point of the cookie tray.

LINZER COOKIES

PREP 40 minutes
CHILL 1 hour
BAKE 6 minutes per batch at 375°F

WHAT YOU NEED

⅓ cup butter, softened
⅓ cup shortening
¾ cup granulated sugar
1½ tsp. baking powder
¼ tsp. salt
¼ tsp. ground cinnamon
⅛ tsp. ground cloves
1 egg
1 Tbsp. milk
½ tsp. lemon zest
½ tsp. vanilla
2 cups all-purpose flour
   Powdered sugar
⅓ to ½ cup raspberry, strawberry, or cherry preserves or jam

WHAT YOU DO

1. In a large bowl beat butter and shortening with a mixer on medium 30 seconds. Add sugar, baking powder, salt, cinnamon, and cloves; beat until combined. Beat in egg, milk, lemon zest, and vanilla. Beat in flour. Divide dough in half. Cover; chill 1 hour or until dough is easy to handle.

2. Preheat oven to 375°F. On a lightly floured surface, roll one dough portion at a time until ⅛ inch thick. Using 2½-inch cookie cutters, cut dough into desired shapes. Place 1 inch apart on an ungreased cookie sheet. Using ¾-inch cookie cutters, cut out centers from half the cookies. Reroll scraps as needed.

3. Bake 6 to 8 minutes or until edges are light brown. Remove; cool on a wire rack.

4. Sift powdered sugar over cookies with cutout centers. Spread bottoms of whole cookies with preserves, using about 1 tsp. for each cookie. Top with powdered sugar-dusted cookies, bottom sides down. Serve within 2 hours. Makes 20 sandwich cookies.

Lemon Poppy Seed Prepare as directed, except omit cinnamon and cloves. Beat in ½ to 1 tsp. poppy seeds with the flour. Substitute lemon curd for the preserves.

Chocolate Marshmallow Prepare as directed, except omit cinnamon, cloves, and lemon zest and reduce flour to 1¼ cups. Beat in ½ cup unsweetened cocoa powder with the flour. Substitute marshmallow creme for the preserves, using 2 to 3 tsp. for each cookie.

Chocolate-Hazelnut Prepare as directed, except omit cloves and lemon zest. Beat in ¼ cup finely chopped toasted hazelnuts with the flour. Substitute unsweetened cocoa powder for the powdered sugar and chocolate-hazelnut spread for the preserves.

Gingerbread Prepare as directed, except reduce granulated sugar to ½ cup, increase cloves to ¼ tsp., and add ¾ tsp. ground ginger with the granulated sugar. Add ⅓ cup molasses with the egg and substitute cider vinegar for the milk. Substitute fig jam or cookie butter for the raspberry preserves.

Churro Prepare as directed, except substitute orange zest for the lemon zest. Substitute a mixture of 2 Tbsp. granulated sugar and 1 tsp. ground cinnamon for the powdered sugar and dulce de leche for the preserves.

STRAWBERRY JAM

GINGERBREAD

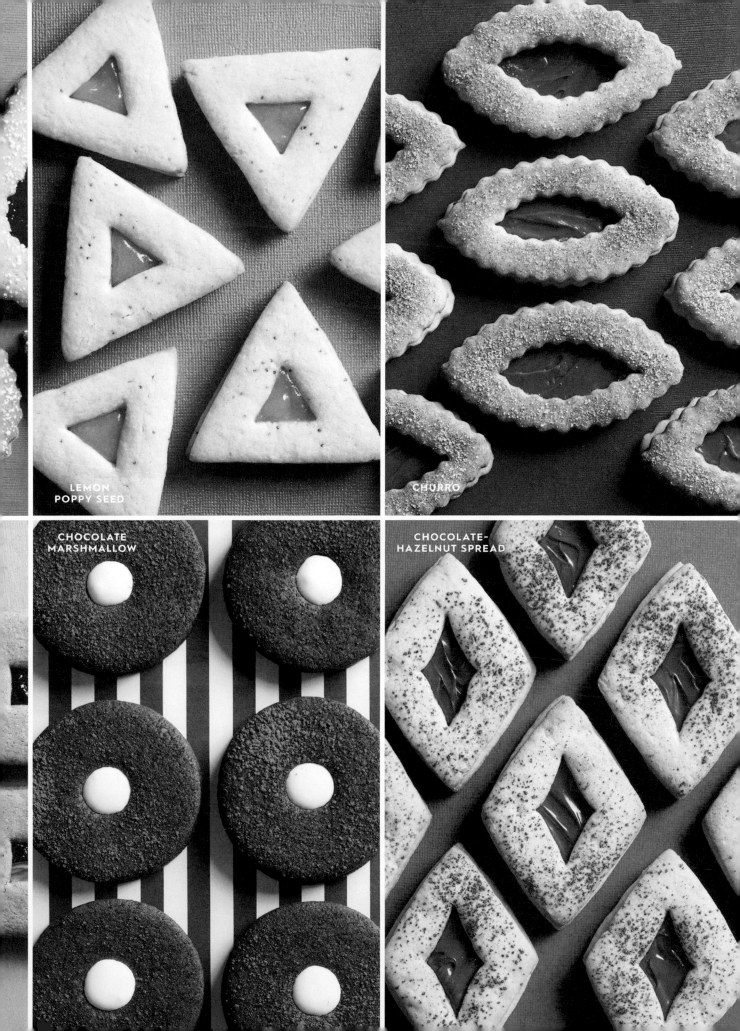

LEMON
POPPY SEED

CHURRO

CHOCOLATE
MARSHMALLOW

CHOCOLATE-
HAZELNUT SPREAD

gifts

SPREAD GOOD CHEER
Craft and cook gifts that
share the joy of the season.

Entertaining Ideas

For family and friends who enjoy the art of entertaining, these gifts are absolute winners.

COLORFUL CUSHION

A multipurpose serving tray is a much-appreciated gift. Put your creative touch on it with a colorful liner made of soft yarns machine-zig-zagged on stiffened felt. Arrange a single layer of fibers on a piece of felt cut to tray size; crazy zig-zag the surface to hold the yarn in place.

BETTER WITH A LETTER

Dress up inexpensive glasses with initials etched permanently into the surfaces. Make a set with the initial signifying your gift recipient's last name or create a glass for each person using their first initial.

WHAT YOU NEED
Drinking glass
Letter sticker
Printer paper
Pencil
Scissors
Tape
Painter's tape
Paintbrush
Etching cream
Dish soap

WHAT YOU DO
1. Place a letter sticker on a glass as shown in Photo A; press down edges firmly.
2. Trace the diamond pattern from page 155 on paper; cut out. Tape the diamond shape on the inside of the glass with the letter in the center as shown in Photo B.
3. On the outside of the glass, use painter's tape to outline the diamond shape as shown in Photo C. Firmly press down the edges.
4. Use a paintbrush to coat the area inside the taped areas with etching cream as shown in Photo D.
5. Let the etching cream dry as directed by the manufacturer. When time is up, rinse off the cream and remove the tape and sticker. Wash the glass with dish soap before using.

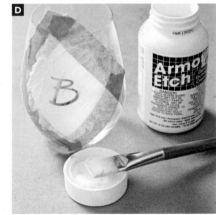

SPOOL SIDE

An industrial-size spool makes a one-of-a-kind side table with one end used as an artist's canvas. Paint one end of the spool and the top of the base with black acrylic paint; let dry. Trace and enlarge the pattern on page 158. Transfer the design to the spool top; paint in the motifs using the photo as a color guide. Let the paint dry. To add the small dots, dip a pencil eraser into black paint and dot onto the surface. Let the paint dry. To protect the surfaces, finish with a clear topcoat; let dry.

HANDLE IT

Personalize a cutting board with a painted design blanketing the handle. Use the pattern on page 154 as a guide or create your own design. Using acrylic paint, start by painting black outlines of desired motifs; let dry. Fill in each area using desired paint colors. Once the paint is dry, brush on a coat of water-base topcoat; let dry. Do not soak the cutting board to clean. Wash the unpainted area with dish soap and dry immediately.

SNACK ATTACK

Plain wood snack dishes transform into super-fun serving pieces with the addition of wood letters. Press-on wood letters make it easy to add a word or phrase to a serving dish. Before removing letters from the backing sheet, paint each needed letter with acrylic paint. Blend in a tiny amount of white paint at the top of each letter; let dry. Press the letters onto the surface of the serving piece.

COASTER BOASTER

Create coasters that have personality plus. Start with plain wood coasters or squares and use a woodburning letter tool to add the word "sip" to one corner. For wood pieces that have a finish, sand the surface before woodburning or the tool may have a tendency to slip. Once the word is burned into the surface, a topcoat can be reapplied

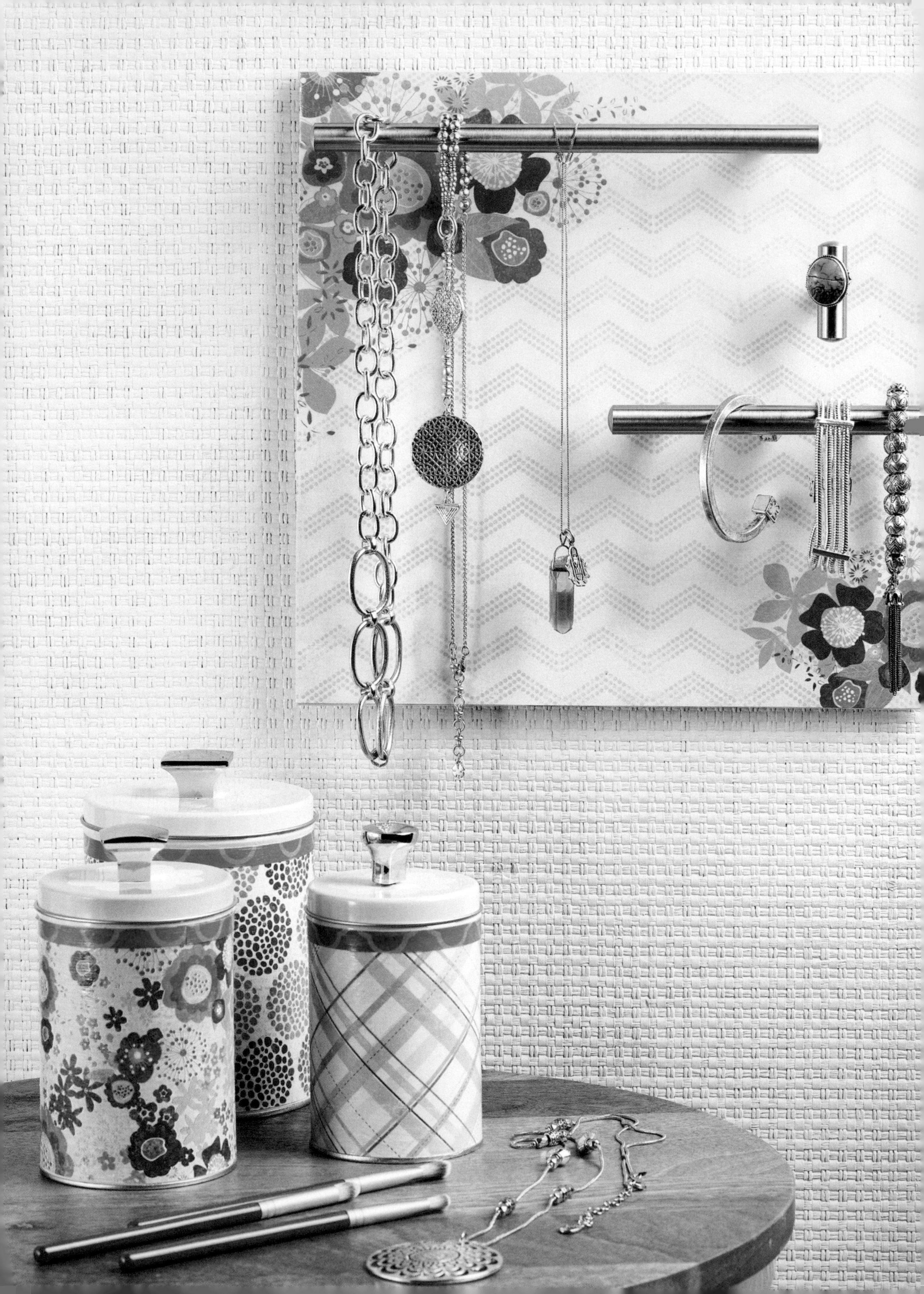

Functional Beauties

Create home or office organizers that can be made in myriad color combinations, patterns, and sizes. What a practical and personal way to show love to your gift recipients.

PRETTY TIDY

Give the gift of organization in a pretty way. To craft this jewelry holder, start with a 12-inch-square piece of ½-inch plywood and a 12-inch-square of scrapbook paper. Coat one side of the plywood with decoupage medium. While wet, carefully align one edge of the scrapbook paper with one edge of the plywood; smooth paper over the surface. Brush a coat of decoupage medium on the front of the paper; let dry. Attach D-style picture hangers to each top corner on the back. Drill holes and attach bar-style drawer pulls and knobs in an arrangement, like that shown, using screws just long enough to go through the wood to securely hold the hardware in place.

RAISE THE BAR

Here's a great gift for that special guy who has everything. A long bar-style pull makes a firm foundation on which to organize ties. To make the holder, start with a 12-inch-square piece of ½-inch plywood and a 12-inch-square of scrapbook paper. Coat one side of the plywood with decoupage medium. While wet, align one edge of the scrapbook paper with one edge of the plywood; smooth paper over the surface. Brush a coat of decoupage medium on the front of the paper; let dry. Attach D-style picture hangers to each top corner on the back. Drill holes and attach the drawer pull parallel to the top edge, using screws just long enough to go through the wood to securely hold the hardware in place.

QUICK CADDY

Before throwing away an empty nut can, consider making it into a desk organizer instead. For little money and time, you can make a useful, appreciated gift. Nut cans with no sharp edges are preferred. Unused pint and quart paint cans work as well. Cover a clean can with decorative paper, adding a paper band or ribbon around the top.

DYNAMIC DUO

A rescued jar and a wood tag will be a guy's best friends with a few artistic touches. Trim a change jar with a band of decorative paper and a coordinating lid insert. To make the key chain, trace around the tag on paper twice, marking the hole; cut out and use a paper punch to make the hole. Brush the wood tag with decoupage medium and press paper Thread the hole with a short length of ball chain.

DOING THE CAN-CAN-CAN

A wonderful accompaniment to the jewelry rack, a cannister trio keeps the organization vibe going strong. Create coordinating cannisters with the addition of scrapbook papers and decorative knobs. Use double-face tape to hold paper to cannister, piecing if needed. Trim at the top with a band of contrasting paper or ribbon. Drill a hole in the center of the lid and attach the knob using a short bolt, adding washers if needed.

Food Gifts

Package delicious homemade treats to deliver throughout the season. Your thoughtfulness will be warmly received.

SMOKED CHEESE CRACKERS

FALLING FLAKES

Cellophane treat bags make giving food gifts easy, even last minute. To make the presentation more special, whitewash wood snowflakes and thread onto the ends of a 10-inch length of ribbon. Use the ribbon to close the filled bag.

SMOKED CHEESE CRACKERS

PREP 20 minutes
CHILL 4 hours
BAKE 12 minutes at 350°F

WHAT YOU NEED
4 oz. smoked blue cheese, crumbed (1 cup)
¼ cup butter, cut into ½-inch cubes
¾ cup all-purpose flour
¼ tsp. black pepper
Kosher salt or smoked salt

WHAT YOU DO
1. Let cheese and butter come to room temperature. In a food processor combine flour, pepper, cheese, and butter. Cover and pulse until mixture forms a ball. Transfer to a lightly floured surface.
2. Shape dough into a 6×1½-inch log. Wrap with plastic wrap and chill 4 to 24 hours or until firm.
3. Preheat oven to 350°F. Line two baking sheets with parchment paper. Using a sharp knife cut dough into ¼-inch-thick slices. Place 1 inch apart on prepared baking sheets. Prick dough with fork tines. Sprinkle crackers with salt.
4. Bake 12 to 13 minutes or until lightly browned. Remove from baking sheets; cool on wire racks. Makes 6 servings .
To store Place crackers in layers separated by waxed paper in an airtight container; cover. Store at room temperature up to 2 days or freeze up to 2 months.

SATURDAY CINNAMON ROLLS

DECORATIVE DUO

Simple, yet showy, these easy packaging ideas provide a merry solution. A paper baking pan makes an instant slipcover for cinnamon rolls baked in a throw-away pan. Accompany the rolls with a doily-trimmed icing bag closed with a twist tie and this combo is ready to deliver. Divide icing between two disposable decorating bags and give with rolls.

SATURDAY CINNAMON ROLLS

PREP 30 minutes
RISE 1 hour
BAKE 25 minutes at 375°F

WHAT YOU NEED
- ½ cup packed brown sugar
- 1 Tbsp. ground cinnamon
- 2 16-oz. loaves frozen white bread dough or sweet roll dough, thawed
- 3 Tbsp. butter, softened
- ¾ cup raisins (optional)
- 1 recipe Creamy Icing

WHAT YOU DO
1. Grease two 9-inch round baking pans. In a small bowl stir together brown sugar and cinnamon; set aside.
2. On a lightly floured surface roll each loaf of dough into a 12×8-inch rectangle. Spread with softened butter and sprinkle with brown sugar mixture, leaving 1 inch unfilled along one of the long sides. If desired, sprinkle with raisins.

3. Tightly roll up, starting from filled long side, and seal seam with fingertips. Cut each log into eight slices; arrange in prepared baking pans. Cover and let rise in a warm place until nearly double in size (about 1 hour).
4. Preheat oven to 375°F. Bake 25 to 30 minutes or until golden. If necessary to prevent overbrowning, cover rolls with foil the last 10 minutes of baking. Cool slightly in pans on wire racks.
5. Drizzle rolls with Creamy Icing; serve warm. Makes 16 servings .
Creamy Icing In a small bowl stir together 1½ cups powdered sugar, 1 tablespoon softened butter, and ½ teaspoon vanilla. Stir in 1 to 2 tablespoons whipping cream or milk, 1 teaspoon at a time, to make an icing of spreading consistency.

SNICKEROONI
BARS

PAPER UNDER GLASS

An inexpensive glass plate gets an extraordinary facelift with the simple addition of a paper doily and napkin. Cut four sections from a doily to fit the corners of a square glass plate. Brush decoupage medium onto the back of the glass plate; immediately press the doily pieces in place, right side facing the glue. Carefully brush the plate bottom with another coat of decoupage medium. Press the patterned side of a paper napkin onto the decoupage medium; trim off excess and let dry.

SNICKEROONI BARS

PREP 30 minutes
BAKE 12 minutes at 350°F
FREEZE 30 minutes
CHILL 2 hours

WHAT YOU NEED

Nonstick cooking spray
1   14.3-oz. pkg. chocolate sandwich cookies with white filling (36 cookies)
⅓   cup butter, melted
1¼ cups sugar
⅓   cup butter
1   5-oz. can evaporated milk
1   7-oz. jar marshmallow creme
¼   cup creamy peanut butter
1¾ cups cocktail peanuts or salted cashews, chopped
1   11-oz. bag vanilla caramels, unwrapped
1½ cups milk chocolate chips (8 oz.)

WHAT YOU DO

1. Preheat oven to 350°F. Line a 13×9-inch baking pan with foil, extending foil over edges of pan. Lightly coat foil with cooking spray. For the crust, place cookies in a food processor. Cover and process until finely chopped. In a bowl mix together cookie crumbs and melted butter. Firmly press crumb mixture into prepared pan. Bake 12 minutes or until set. Cool in pan on wire rack.
2. For the nougat, in a medium saucepan combine sugar, ⅓ cup butter, and ½ cup evaporated milk. Bring to boiling over medium-high heat, stirring to dissolve sugar. Reduce heat to medium. Simmer, uncovered, 10 minutes. Remove from heat. Stir in marshmallow creme and peanut butter until smooth. Stir in peanuts. Pour nougat over crust, spreading to edges. Place pan in freezer 20 minutes while preparing caramel layer.
3. For caramel layer, place caramels and remaining evaporated milk in a microwave-safe bowl. Microwave 1½ to 2 minutes or until caramels are melted, stirring every 30 seconds. Pour caramel mixture over nougat layer, spreading to edges. Return pan to freezer 10 minutes.
4. In a small microwave-safe bowl heat chocolate chips 1 minute or until melted, stirring every 30 seconds. Pour chocolate over caramel layer, spreading to edges. Cover and chill 2 hours or until firm. Use foil to lift uncut bars out of pan. Cut into bars. Makes 60 servings.

CARDAMOM-CLEMENTINE SYRUP

CARDAMOM-CLEMENTINE SYRUP

PREP 15 minutes
CHILL 48 hours

WHAT YOU NEED

2   clementines or 1 orange
½   cup sugar
½   cup water
2   Tbsp. green cardamom pods

WHAT YOU DO

1. Using a vegetable peeler, cut peel from clementines, avoiding the white pith. (Reserve fruit for another use.)
2. In a small saucepan combine peel, sugar, water, and cardamom pods. Bring to boiling; reduce heat. Simmer until sugar dissolves, stirring constantly.
3. Cool syrup completely; transfer to a bowl. Cover; chill 48 hours. Remove cardamom and peel. Makes 24 servings.

BOTTLE BOBBLES

Dress up bottles so they're ready for gift giving in a flash. Wrap the bottle neck with a length of 1-inch-wide ribbon; cut leaving overlapping tails and notch the ends. Overlap the ribbon ends as shown; add a dot of hot glue to adhere the layers together. Add a trio of short greenery pieces as well as three mini ornaments to the center. Slip the ribbon embellishment over the neck of the bottle.

CHOW-DOWN
SWEET AND SALTY
SNACK MIX

QUICK CONES

Paper plates offer an array of holiday patterns to make sturdy cones for holding snack mix. Using pinking shears, cut a large paper plate in half. Round one point and trim off the remaining plate edge. Use a long-reach paper punch to make two holes, ½ inch apart, on the rounded edge as shown by the bow placement, left. Hot-glue trim to the back side of the cut edge. Fold plate into a triangle as shown and mark the whole punches on the layer underneath; punch holes where marked. Thread narrow ribbon through the holes; tie a bow on the front. Fill a cellophane treat bag with snack mix. Close the bag with a twist tie.

CHOW-DOWN SWEET AND SALTY SNACK MIX

START TO FINISH 20 minutes

WHAT YOU NEED

7   cups bite-size corn square cereal
     and/or puffed corn cereal
2   cups pretzel sticks
1   cup salted peanuts
½   cup creamy peanut butter
½   cup semisweet chocolate pieces
½   cup dark chocolate pieces
¼   cup butter
1   tsp. vanilla
1⅓ cups powdered sugar

WHAT YOU DO

1. In an extra-large bowl combine cereal, pretzels, and peanuts. In a large microwave-safe bowl combine peanut butter, semisweet chocolate, dark chocolate, and butter. Microwave 30 to 60 seconds or until chocolate is melted, stirring every 20 seconds.
2. Stir vanilla into chocolate mixture. Pour chocolate mixture over cereal mixture, stirring quickly to coat evenly.
3. In a 2-gallon resealable plastic bag combine cereal mixture and powdered sugar. Seal bag; shake to coat. Spread mix on parchment paper or foil; cool completely. Makes 18 servings.

SAVORY
WALNUTS

TISSUE PAPER TOPPERS

Whether giving a single serving or enough for a whole family to enjoy, this packaging idea works for any size tin. Wrap the tin with a double layer of ribbons; tape on the bottom. For the topper, thread three jingle bells into the center of a 6-inch piece of wire; twist to secure. Layer nine sheets of tissue paper; trace around the lid onto the top sheet. Cut out the tissue paper circles using pinking shears. Accordion-fold the tissue paper layers, pinch in the center, and secure with the wired jingle bells. Hot-glue the trim to the center of the ribbon.

SAVORY WALNUTS

PREP 10 minutes
BAKE 12 minutes at 350°F

WHAT YOU NEED
- 2 cups walnut halves
- 2 Tbsp. Worcestershire-style marinade for chicken
- 1 Tbsp. olive oil
- 2 tsp. snipped fresh thyme or ½ tsp. dried thyme, crushed
- 1 tsp. snipped fresh rosemary or ¼ tsp. dried rosemary, crushed
- ¼ tsp. salt
- ⅛ tsp. cayenne pepper

WHAT YOU DO
1. Preheat oven to 350°F. Spread walnuts in an even layer in a 13×9-inch baking pan. In a bowl combine remaining ingredients. Drizzle over nuts; toss gently to coat.
2. Bake 12 to 15 minutes or until nuts are toasted, stirring occasionally. Spread nuts on foil; cool completely. Makes 8 servings.

FLIP A LID

Seasonal touches dress up a jar with ease.
Start by hot-gluing a glittered pinecone in
the center of the lid. Tuck in mini pinecones,
faux berries, and a pair of leaves cut from
plaid paper (pattern on page 156).

CRANBERRY
CHUTNEY

CRANBERRY CHUTNEY

PREP 20 minutes
COOK 10 minutes

WHAT YOU NEED

1	navel orange
¾	cup packed brown sugar
¼	cup cider vinegar
¼	cup water
⅓	cup finely chopped red onion
4	¼-inch-thick slices fresh ginger
1	tsp. mustard seeds
¼	tsp. salt
⅛	tsp. crushed red pepper
1	12-oz. pkg. fresh cranberries, rinsed
1	Granny Smith apple, peeled and chopped

WHAT YOU DO

1. Remove 2 teaspoons zest from orange; set aside. Cut ¼ inch from top and bottom of orange. Use a sharp knife to remove skin and pith from orange. Working over a medium saucepan (to catch juice), separate and remove segments from orange. Cut segments into small pieces; set aside. Squeeze membrane over pan to remove remaining juice.

2. Add brown sugar, vinegar, water, onion, ginger, mustard seeds, salt, and crushed red pepper to saucepan. Bring to boiling over medium-high heat. Add cranberries and orange zest. Return to boiling; reduce heat. Cook, uncovered, 7 minutes, stirring occasionally. Add apple; cook 3 minutes or until apple is just tender.

3. Remove pan from heat; remove and discard ginger. Stir in reserved orange segments. Serve warm or refrigerate, covered, up to 2 days. Bring to room temperature before serving if chilled. Makes 6 servings.

COOKIE CRACKERS

This easy-to-do packaging, made from scrapbook or wrapping paper, can be playful or elegant, depending on the pattern. Cut a 6×10-inch piece of clear food-safe cellophane; place lengthwise on surface. Stack a dozen cookies. Lay the cookie stack on the cellophane lengthwise. Roll the cellophane around the cookies; tape in center to secure. Twist each cellophane end; secure with a twist tie. Cut two coordinating pieces of paper, 8×3½ inches and 8×2½ inches. Center the small paper on top of the larger one, wrap around cookie stack, tape to secure.

PISTACHIO
CRANBERRY
ICEBOX COOKIES

PISTACHIO CRANBERRY ICEBOX COOKIES

PREP 25 minutes
CHILL 2 hours
BAKE 10 minutes at 350°F
COOL 1 minute

WHAT YOU NEED

¾	cup unsalted butter, softened
⅓	granulated sugar
½	tsp. ground cinnamon
½	tsp. orange zest
¼	tsp. salt
1½	cups all-purpose flour
¾	finely chopped pistachio nuts
⅓	cup snipped dried cranberries
¼	cup coarse sugar

WHAT YOU DO

1. In a large bowl beat butter with a mixer on medium to high 30 seconds. Add sugar, cinnamon, zest, and salt. Beat 3 minutes or until light and fluffy. Reduce speed to low. Gradually beat in as much flour as you can with mixer. Stir in remaining flour. Stir in ½ cup nuts and cranberries; use hands to knead dough until smooth.

2. Divide dough in half. Shape each half into an 8½-inch log. In a bowl combine coarse sugar and ¼ cup nuts. Roll logs in sugar-nut mixture. Wrap each log in plastic wrap or waxed paper. Chill 2 hours or until dough is firm enough to slice (1 to 2 hours in refrigerator or 30 minutes in freezer).

3. Preheat oven to 350°F. Line cookie sheets with parchment paper. Use a serrated knife to cut logs into ¼-inch slices; place 1 inch apart on cookie sheets.

4. Bake 10 to 12 minutes or until edges are just starting to brown. Cool on cookie sheets 1 minute. Transfer to wire racks to cool completely. Makes 60 servings.

Box Tops

JINGLE BELLS ROCK

Make a wrapped gift extra special with velvet ribbon loops cushioning a trio of jingle bells. Choose two colors of ribbon to coordinate with the wrap and cross them in one corner; tape or hot-glue on the back. Use hot glue to attach ribbon loops and jingle bells to the intersection.

QUICK STICK

Paper poinsettia stickers add a pretty touch to layered ribbons. The scrapbook section of a crafts store offers endless possibilities for dimensional embellishments. If they won't adhere to the ribbon, use a dot of hot glue to hold the m in place.

SO NATURAL

Printed kraft paper creates the perfect backdrop for a pair of elongated pinecones. Choose a coordinating pair of ribbons to top the wrapped package, one wide and one thin, and secure around the package, tying narrow ribbon into a bow on the top. Hot-glue a grouping of faux berries and mini pinecones to the bow's center with the large pinecones trailing below it.

ORNAMENTED

Here's a wrap idea that's a gift in itself. Choose a gift wrap that complements an ornament; wrap the gift box. Set the box on end and tie a ribbon bow around the edge. Hang a Christmas tree ornament from the bow.

SHOWSTOPPER

A large glittered snowflake makes a beautiful focal point for a gift top. Tie a ribbon bow horizontally across the top of the package. Tie a snowflake ornament to the ribbon underneath the bow.

kids

Make memories with the kids crafting trims and treasures that brighten the season.

All Buttoned Up

Pinned, sewed, or glued, buttons can be used to create all sorts of holiday decorations. Use your imagination—and buttons in all your favorite colors— to make merry adornments.

SEW SPECIAL

Help with holiday giftwrapping by making extra-special ribbons and bows. Basic stitches and mismatched buttons make the most of ribbon remnants. Use embroidery floss to sew buttons onto ribbon or to the center of a bow. Choose buttons and floss that coordinate with giftwrap.

DOTS AGLOW

Button polka dots give a bright finish to a snowy white pillar candle. For each dot, poke a short map pin through the holes in stacked buttons and push carefully into the wax. Keep adding buttons until the surface is covered, leaving space between the buttons.

Never leave burning candles unattended.

COOL COMBINATION

Get out the button box and use your imagination to create a snowy friend to enjoy all winter long. Paint an 11×14-inch canvas with light blue acrylic paint; let dry. Trace the pattern on page 157 and transfer to the canvas as a placement guide. Working in a small area at a time, coat the area with crafts glue. Press buttons into the glue, using the photo as a color guide. Finish the base layer first; add top layer.

DECK THE BALLS

Arranged in rows or in patterns, buttons bring a joyful touch to plain plastic ornaments. If desired, start with a ribbon hot-glued to the surface. Using the photos as inspiration, hot-glue buttons onto the ornament.

PRETTY PRESENTATION

They're so cute, gift recipients will want to keep these little treasures. To make a gift tag, fold a small piece of cardstock in half; punch a hole at the top and thread with cord. Cut a smaller piece of white cardstock, approximately 1 inch smaller all around. Use hot glue or thick crafts glue to attach buttons in the desired pattern. Let dry. Use a glue stick to adhere decorated piece to contrasting paper; trim a narrow border and adhere to the cardstock tag.

FROSTY GOODNESS

When it's time for holiday cupcakes, let your artistic creations dance across the frosting. Using a crafts stick as the base, hot-glue two white buttons onto one end of the stick. Hot-glue a tiny red or orange button in the center of the top button for a nose. To make the eyes and mouth, dip a toothpick into black acrylic paint and dot onto the button; let dry. Glue two tiny buttons on the bottom. Use felt or fleece to make the hat and scarf. Cut a narrow strip for the scarf, tie around the snowman and trim the ends. Cut a triangle for a hat, trim with a contrasting band, and top with a button.

It's About Tine

Here's a crafting idea that gets right to the point. Use a fork in lieu of a paintbrush to make fun patterns with paint on paper.

SEASON'S GREETINGS

Teachers, family, and friends will love getting handmade cards you create. For the background, cut a 4¾-inch square from white paper. To make the wreath shape, dip fork tines into green paint. Make a crisscross design in a donut shape as demonstrated in Photos A and B; let dry. Dip the tine ends in red and pink paint; dot onto wreath to indicate berries and let dry. Tie a multiribbon bow; hot-glue to wreath. Use a glue stick to adhere the wreath to a 5-inch square of green paper. Glue the design atop a 5¾-inch card folded from cardstock.

QUICK NOTE

You can make cards for everyone you love with this easy-to-paint greenery sprig design. On a 4-inch white cardstock square, use a black marking pen to draw two arches as shown in Photo A. Dip a fork into green paint and draw curved pine needles along the curved lines as shown in Photo B. Add green dot accents and berries as shown in Photo C. Let the paint dry. Use a glue stick to adhere the design to a 4⅝-inch piece of contrasting paper. Glue the design to a 5-inch card folded from cardstock.

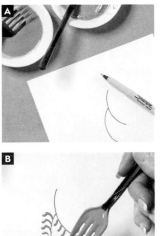

FORK IT OVER

Put your mark on plain white paper to make one-of-a-kind gift wrap. To make lines, press paint-dipped fork tines onto the paper as shown in Photo A. To make crosshatches, use a fork to create lines in one direction, then the other in an X formation as shown in Photo B. To make blotched motifs, after making crosshatches, press a clean sheet of paper on top and peel off as shown in Photo C. To make dots, dip a fork into paint and press onto the paper as shown in Photo D.

SPECIAL DELIVERY

Share some holiday treats with handmade paper cones as
the festive carrier. Trace the pattern on page 158; use the
pattern to cut a cone shape from white cardstock. To make
the lines, dip a fork into paint and lay it onto the paper as
shown in Photo A. Use a different fork for each paint color,
alternating colors. Make several rows until the entire paper
is covered; let dry. Shape the paper into a cone shape; use
hot glue to hold the shape intact. Trim the scallop edge with
pom-poms.

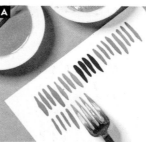

VERY MERRY MITTEN

Make mittens in all your favorite colors. No knitting required. Trace the pattern on page 158; cut out. Use the pattern to cut a mitten shape from white cardstock. Use a fork dipped into paint to make the crosshatch pattern on the mitten as shown in Photo A. Make lines on the cuff as shown in Photo B. Make rows of dots between the lines by dipping the tine tips in paint and dotting on the paper. Let the paint dry. Use a glue stick to adhere the painted mitten to white cardstock; trim a narrow border. Punch a hole in the left side of the cuff. Hot-glue trim and jingle bells to the ornament.

PRACTICE ROUND

Paint and pom-poms is all it takes to make a showy napkin ring from a plain paper band. For each napkin ring, cut a 1¼×7-inch piece of white cardstock. Or use a full sheet of paper for painting and cut into strips when dry. Using the various fork painting techniques as shown on pages 146–149, make designs on the paper strips or sheet. Have fun trying different ways to make paint designs using fork tines. Let dry. If painting was done on a full sheet of paper, cut into the strips. Hot-glue pom-poms in a row in the center of the band. Shape the band into a ring; tape ends together.

Playful Pom-Poms

TAG A BAG

Decorate fun treat bags for friends by adding mini pom-poms to polka-dot goodie bags. Using the photo for ideas, dot thick crafts glue in a pattern on each bag; place pom-poms on glue and let dry.

IT'S A STRING THING

Whether strung across your bedroom or from a tree limb to limb, these playful garlands bring good cheer. Thread a darning needle with yarn. Poke the needle through the center of different size pom-poms, spacing as desired. To add bows, cut narrow strips of fleece and tie onto the yarn between two pom-poms. Trim the fleece ends to look like a bow tie.

OUT ON A LIMB

Craft a snowy clan that brings charm to a tabletop tree. A pom-pom pair makes the base for a snowman in no time. Thread embroidery floss through the center of a mini pom-pom, 1-inch fleece circle, and two large white pom-poms; run floss back in reverse order and knot ends for a hanger. Make French knot (see diagram on page 158) eyes and a nose from black and orange embroidery floss, starting and ending the floss under the hat. Tie a narrow piece of fleece around the center as a scarf; fringe the ends. Glue tiny pom-poms on the front for buttons.

DRESS-UP CUP

Brighten your Christmas table with festive favors for everyone who's gathered around it. Trace the holly pattern on page 154. Use the pattern to cut two leaves from green paper. Use a glue stick to adhere the leaves to turquoise paper; trim a narrow border. Hot-glue the leaves to a paper treat cup, adding three pom-pom berries. Fill each cup with paper shred, adding holiday candies on top.

FILL 'ER UP

Let your favorite colors shine with the help of clear plastic ornaments. Thread the hanger with a short length of yarn; knot ends. Remove the hanger and fill the ornament with mini pom-poms, layering if desired. Snap on the hanger cap and the ornament is tree ready.

patterns

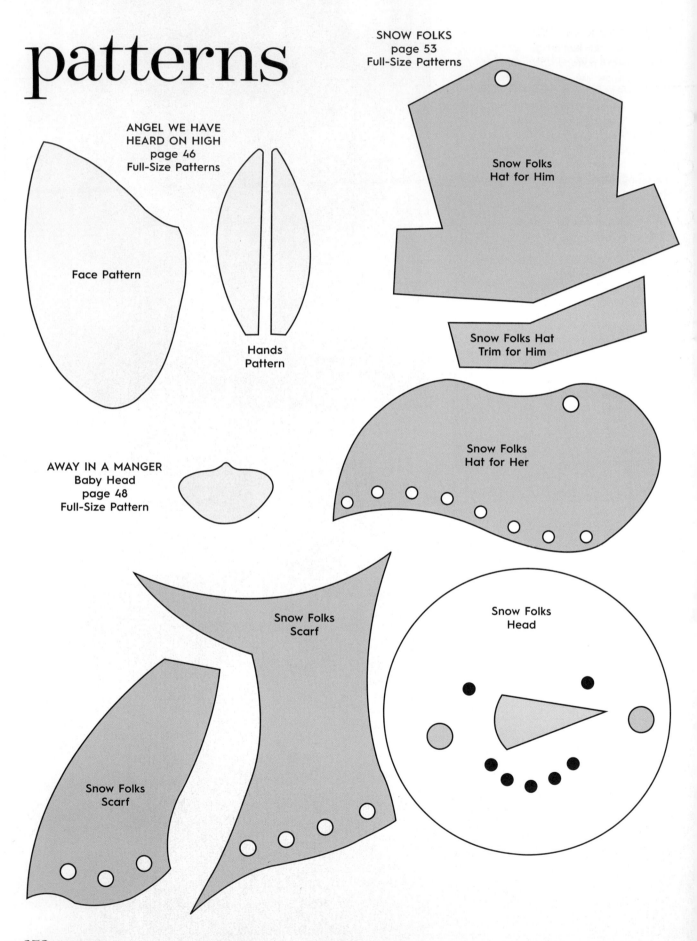

ANGEL WE HAVE
HEARD ON HIGH
page 46
Full-Size Patterns

Face Pattern

Hands
Pattern

AWAY IN A MANGER
Baby Head
page 48
Full-Size Pattern

SNOW FOLKS
page 53
Full-Size Patterns

Snow Folks
Hat for Him

Snow Folks Hat
Trim for Him

Snow Folks
Hat for Her

Snow Folks
Scarf

Snow Folks
Scarf

Snow Folks
Head

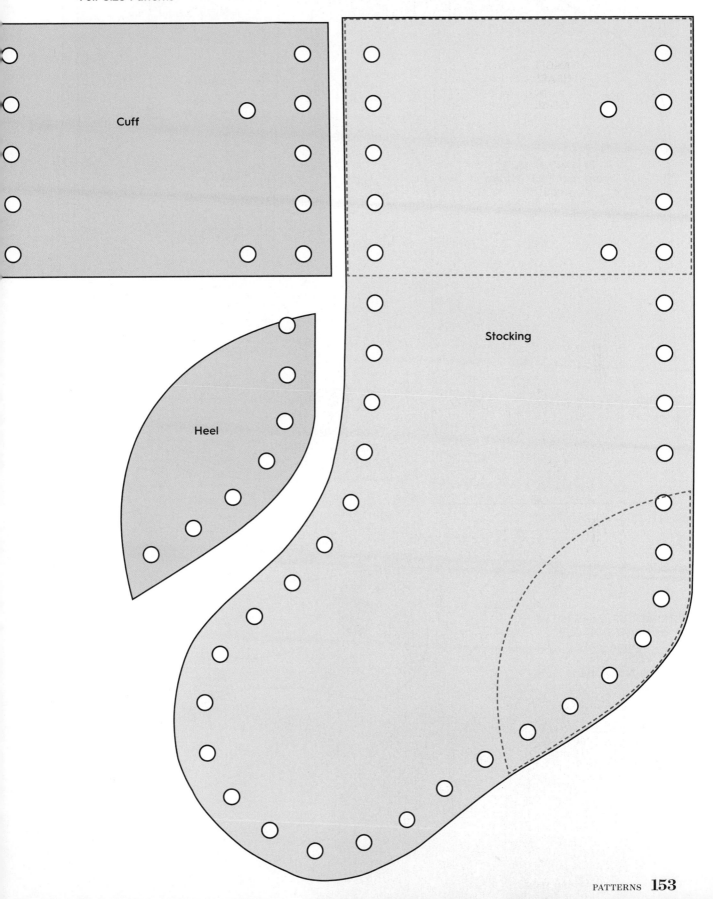

Cuff

Stocking

Heel

Patterns

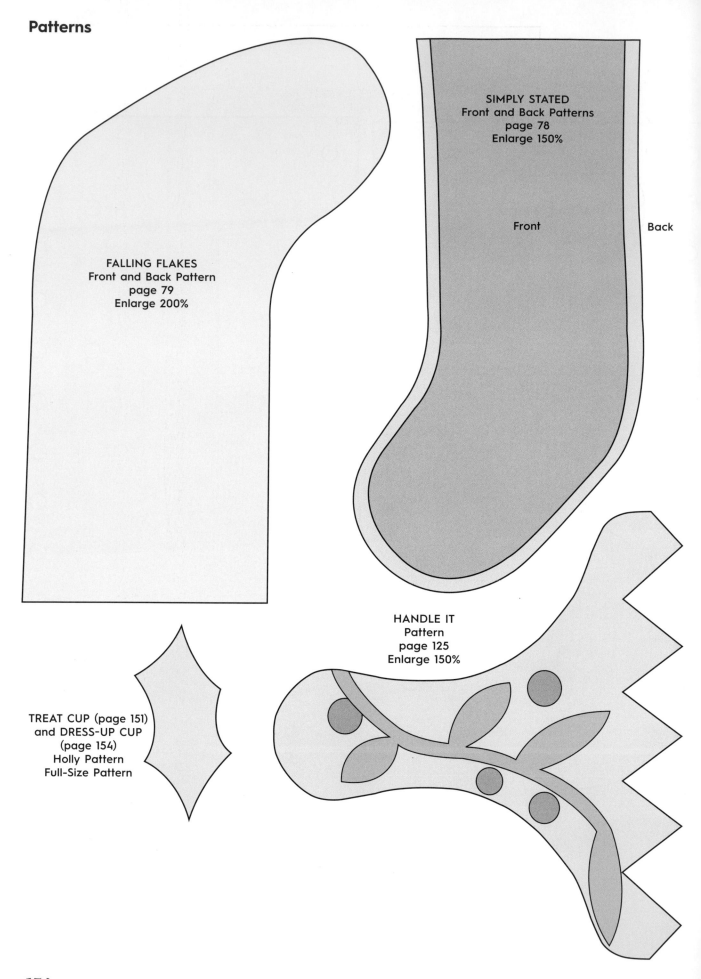

FALLING FLAKES
Front and Back Pattern
page 79
Enlarge 200%

SIMPLY STATED
Front and Back Patterns
page 78
Enlarge 150%

Front   Back

HANDLE IT
Pattern
page 125
Enlarge 150%

TREAT CUP (page 151)
and DRESS-UP CUP
(page 154)
Holly Pattern
Full-Size Pattern

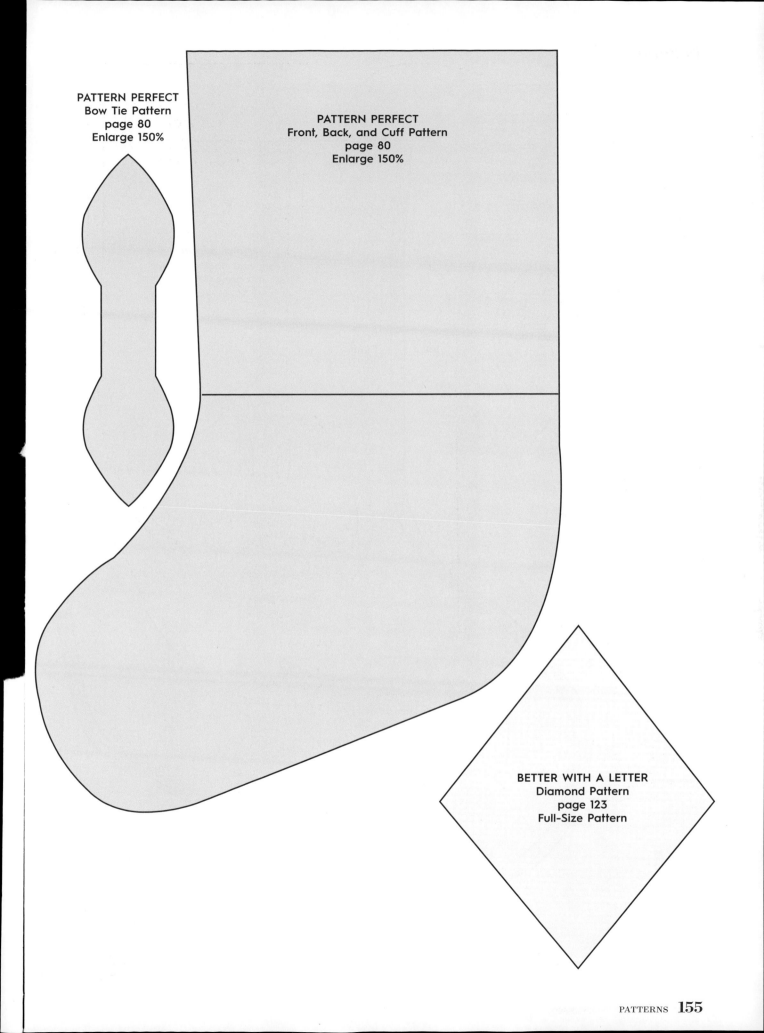

PATTERN PERFECT
Bow Tie Pattern
page 80
Enlarge 150%

PATTERN PERFECT
Front, Back, and Cuff Pattern
page 80
Enlarge 150%

BETTER WITH A LETTER
Diamond Pattern
page 123
Full-Size Pattern

Patterns

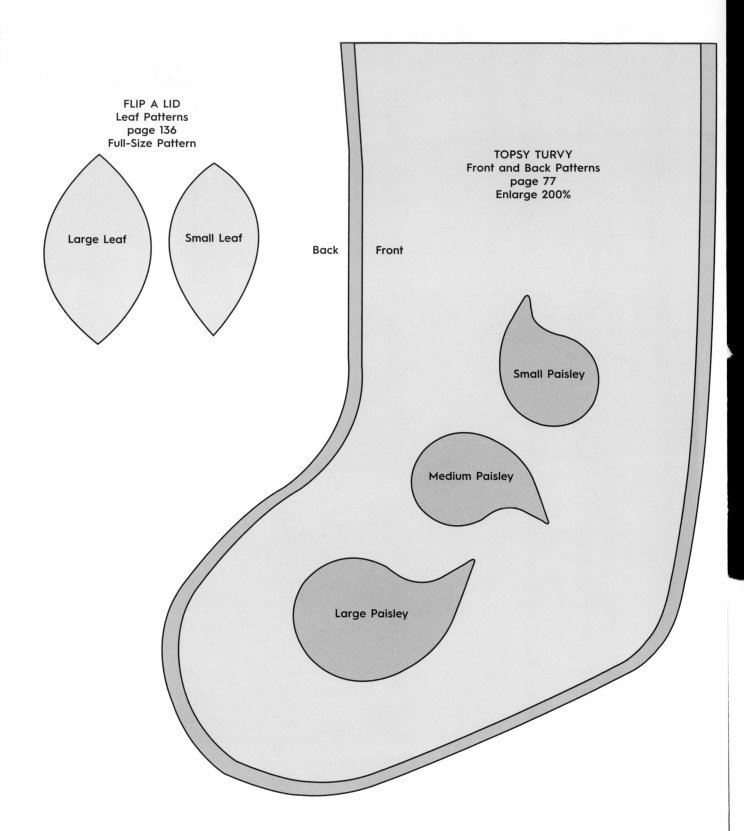

FLIP A LID
Leaf Patterns
page 136
Full-Size Pattern

Large Leaf

Small Leaf

TOPSY TURVY
Front and Back Patterns
page 77
Enlarge 200%

Back   Front

Small Paisley

Medium Paisley

Large Paisley

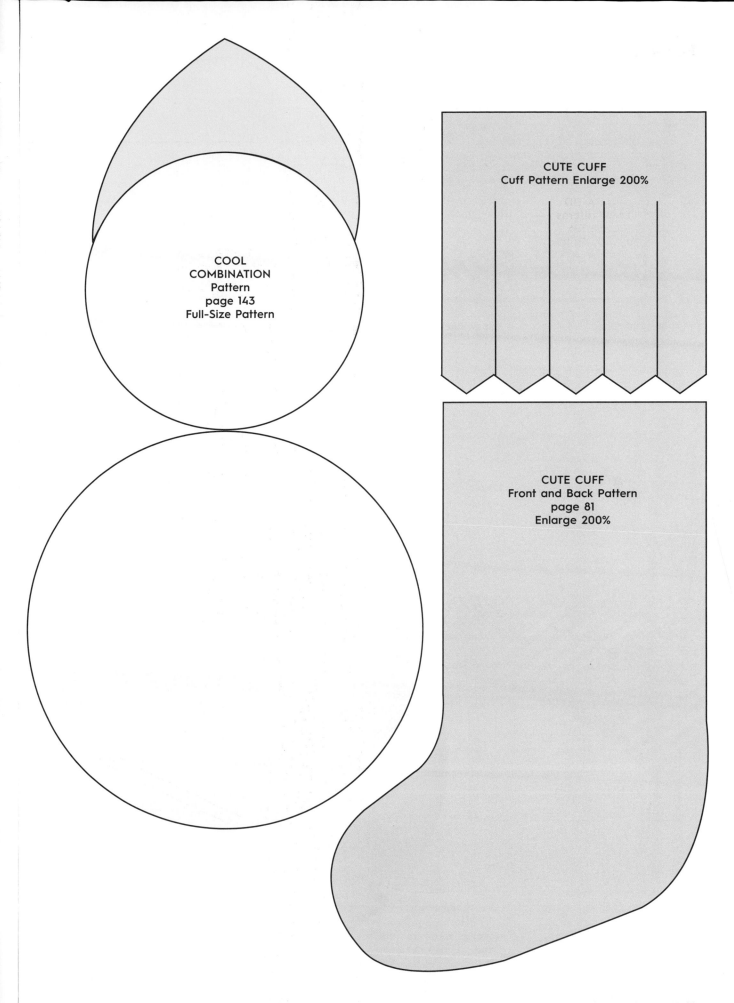

COOL
COMBINATION
Pattern
page 143
Full-Size Pattern

CUTE CUFF
Cuff Pattern Enlarge 200%

CUTE CUFF
Front and Back Pattern
page 81
Enlarge 200%

Patterns

EMBROIDERY STITCH DIAGRAMS

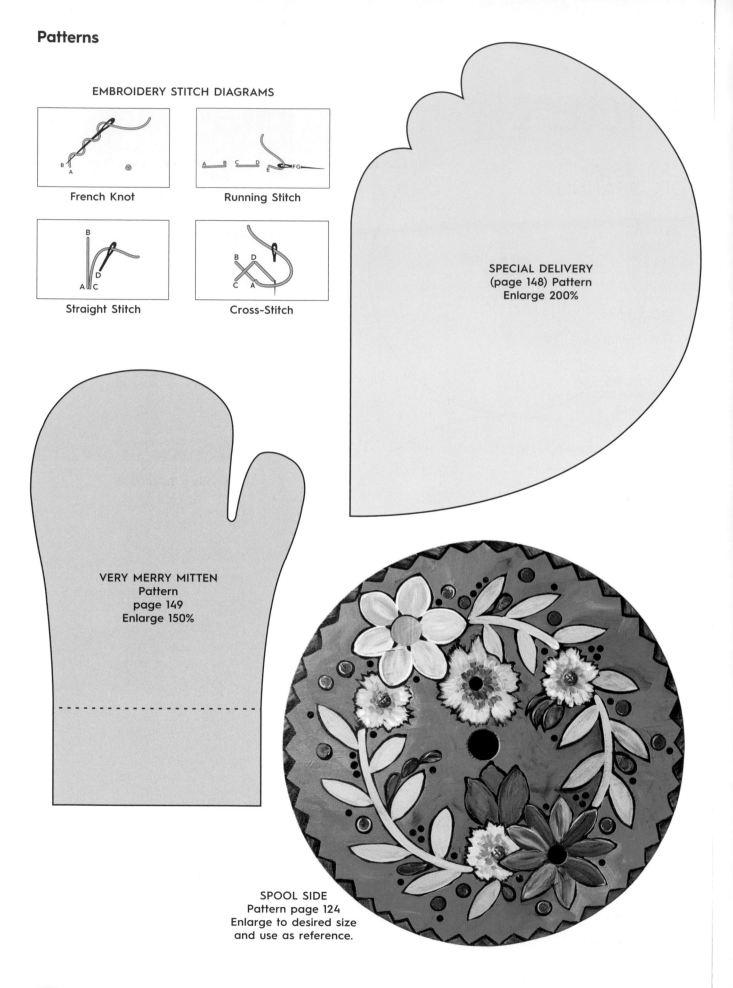

French Knot

Running Stitch

Straight Stitch

Cross-Stitch

SPECIAL DELIVERY
(page 148) Pattern
Enlarge 200%

VERY MERRY MITTEN
Pattern
page 149
Enlarge 150%

SPOOL SIDE
Pattern page 124
Enlarge to desired size
and use as reference.

index

Index

CREDITS

Photo Styling
Sue Banker
Doug Samuelson

Photography
Marty Baldwin
Jason Donnelly
Jacob Fox
Blaine Moats
Brie Passano